CW00432730

THE
JUICE
2009

The Juice 2009
by Matt Skinner

The Juice Team and Mitchell Beazley would like to send a big thank you to all the wine merchants, agents, retailers, and producers who helped with the research for this edition of the book.

First published in Great Britain in 2008 by Mitchell Beazley, an imprint of Octopus Publishing Group Ltd, 2–4 Heron Quays, London E14 4JP. www.octopusbooks.co.uk

An Hachette Livre UK Company www.hachettelivre.co.uk

ISBN 978 1 84533 469 7

A CIP catalogue record for this book is available from the British Library.

Set in Helvetica

Colour reproduction by AltaImages in the UK
Printed and bound by R R Donnelley in China

The author and publishers will be grateful for any information which will assist them in keeping future editions up-to-date. Although all reasonable care has been taken in the preparation of this book, neither the publishers nor the author can accept any liability for any consequences arising from the use thereof, or the information contained therein.

Commissioning Editor: Rebecca Spry
Managing Editor: Hilary Lumsden
Project Editor: Leanne Bryan
Copy-editor: Samantha Stokes
Proofreader: Susan Keevil
Deputy Art Director: Yasia Williams-Leedham
Concept Design: Matt Utber
Layout Design: Eoghan O'Brien
Photographer: Chris Terry
Production Manager: Peter Hunt

Price key

These prices are to be used as a guide only

$	Under $10
$$	$10–20
$$$	$21–30
$$$$	$31–100
$$$$$	Over $100

Contents

Welcome 4

How It All Works 6

The Juice Awards 8

    Wine of the Year 9

    Bargain of the Year 9

    Producer of the Year 10

Varieties, Places, and Styles 11

The Hot 100 20

    Drink 20 wines for drinking now 22

    Give 20 wines for putting smiles on faces 56

    Dine 20 wines to drink with food 90

    Splurge 20 wines to blow the rent on 122

    Stash 20 wines for drinking later 154

Stockists 188

Cheers 192

Welcome

With the health of our planet in pretty dire shape, and the wine industry braced to feel the effects of climate change long before most, I thought that this year would be as good a time as any to look at the efforts and initiatives of those producers working against the odds to make a difference. Producers who are working to make packaging lighter, to build and develop energy efficient wineries, to conserve water, and to grow and produce in the most natural way possible. Producers who are trying to leave things in a better shape than they found them in. Producers who I believe are worthy of your support.

The more research I did for this year's edition, the more I got thinking about what we do to produce the book, and how we might do it more efficiently. For starters, we cut out all of the travel that was undertaken to produce the photography for previous editions. Instead we just gathered up our gear and walked around the block to Holborn Studios, where we laid out a giant collage of every photograph we'd ever taken. We then put up a huge ladder and made Chris Terry climb to the top and take even more lovely photos of, well, all of his lovely photos. It was a beautiful thing and these pictures form the basis for the images you'll find over the coming pages.

I also learned that there are plenty more things I could be doing to make this process a little kinder on Mother Nature. Don't get me wrong: just because I've made a few small changes, by no means do I think I'm perfect, but it's a start, and like many of the producers I've included in this year's guide, I'm committed to making more changes as we go forward.

Matt

How It All Works

What began life as a weekly email sent out to friends and workmates in a vain attempt to help them drink better, has now become a regular distillation of my drinking year. As with previous editions, The Juice 2009 combines 100 wine recommendations together with a few handy tips and a little bit of wisdom. Think of it as the big kids' survival guide to Planet Wine, or better still, a huge step toward better drinking.

So here's the drill. I thought that rather than ranking the wines 1 to 100, it'd be far more useful if I grouped the wines by occasion, and so as with previous years I've split our 100 wines into five easy groups of 20 wines each: DRINK, GIVE, DINE, SPLURGE, and STASH. There's something here for everyone: every taste, every budget, and every occasion.

As per last year, I've made every effort to ensure that both price and vintage (the current release has been reviewed wherever possible) are as accurate as possible at the time of publication. Listed stockists are a mixture of supermarkets, national chains, smaller independent wine retailers, and online merchants – the idea being that you should be able to get your hands on most of the following 100 wines without too much heartache.

Happy drinking!

The Juice Awards

Awards time always brings about a certain sense of dread. For starters, there is very deliberately no ranking system in *The Juice*: there are no star ratings and no scores out of 100. Pedestals are not what this guide has ever been about. Irrespective of price, each of the wines featured in this book deserves to be here for one reason or another. That said, throughout the course of the year, there are always one or two wines and one or two names that repeatedly crop up, and so for that reason I think it's important you know who and what these stellar achievers are. So, without apology, these are the wines that I talked about, enthused about, and repeatedly sniffed, swirled, and slurped this year.

WINE OF THE YEAR

Isole e Olena Cepparello 2003
Tuscany, Italy

Paulo de Marchi's meticulous approach and incredible attention to detail have seen his estate's flagship wine, Cepparello, grow to develop a much-deserved, near cult-like international following. Dreamed up by de Marchi in the late 1970s, Cepparello is assembled from the very best parcels of estate-grown Sangiovese from vineyards perched around 400 metres above sea level. The resulting wines are characterized by incredible depth and purity, and an uncanny ability to age. From the vintage produced during the blisteringly-hot summer of 2003, this example illustrates how, even in the toughest of years, great producers will still make great wines. The end result is spellbinding. Walk over hot coals, sell vital organs, do whatever it takes to get your hands on this incredible wine.

BARGAIN OF THE YEAR

De Bortoli Gulf Station
Pinot Noir 2007
Yarra Valley, Australia

This is ridiculously cheap and yet phenomenally good Pinot Noir. De Bortoli has really raised the bar with this cracking example that effortlessly ticks all of the right boxes. For starters you get terrific varietal character: sweet cherry, smoke, and spice coupled with silky mouth-feel and bright acidity. There's even a small lick of attractive French oak in there just to really add insult to injury. It's all there, and largely thanks to the men behind the controls, Steve Webber and Bill Downie. A cracking wine that just goes from strength to strength.

PRODUCER OF THE YEAR

De Bortoli Wines
Australia

De Bortoli are on quite a roll at the moment. With much recent attention given to their Yarra Valley operation, it would seem that the quality of pretty much everything in the company portfolio – that includes 25 different brands sourced from a similar number of varieties and regions – has also risen in the process. And that's no mean feat. In all, three De Bortoli wines grace the pages of this year's guide, their Gulf Station Pinot Noir 2007 taking the award for Bargain of the Year. And, while much has changed (and grown) since De Bortoli's inception in 1928, the best thing about this family-owned operation is that it has never lost sight of its market, nor forgotten that great wine is made in the vineyard.

Varieties, Places, and Styles

Wine comes in all different shapes and sizes; big wines, little wines, fat wines, skinny wines, good wines, great wines, and wines that will absolutely blow your mind. And while what happens in the winery can play a big role in determining how a wine might end up tasting, grape variety, place, and style will all have an impact too. With the number of varieties and styles now running well into the four figures, here's a brief run-down of those that grace the pages of this year's edition of *The Juice*.

THE WHITES

Chablis (*SHA-blee*)

Chablis is the name of a town in the northern-most part of Burgundy in France. The area's ancient Kimmeridgian limestone soils are unique and produce fine, pristine, mineral-like white wines, made out of Burgundy's white star, Chardonnay. With the use of new oak largely frowned upon in Chablis, the best examples display soft stone/citrus fruit, honey, river-rock, hay, mineral, and cashew character. Trademark mouthwatering acidity ensures the best examples are with us for years.

Chardonnay (*SHAR-do-nay*)

Love it or loathe it, you can't deny this grape its place in wine's hall of fame. Some of the very best examples hail from Burgundy, where texture, finesse, structure, and ageing ability rule over simple "drink-now" fruit flavours. You see, Chardonnay comes in all different shapes and sizes. Flavours range from the delicate, citrus, and slightly honeyed styles of Chablis to warmer, Southern-hemisphere styles, where aromas range from peaches and pears to full-throttle, ripe, tropical fruits like banana, pineapple, guava, and mango.

Chenin Blanc (*shuh-NIN BLAHN*)

Handier than a Swiss army knife, the globetrotting Chenin's high natural acidity and tendency to flirt with botrytis lend it equally well to a variety of styles: sweet, dry, or fizzy. A good traveller, Chenin's stomping ground is France's Loire Valley, where it makes racy dry whites, luscious sweet wines, and clean, frothy fizz. Expect aromas of apples, gooseberries, and fresh herbs.

Gewurztraminer
(*geh-VERZ-trah-MEE-ner*)
Like a drag queen with too much make-up and perfume (and little shame), this is the incredibly camp member of the white-grape family. In reality, Gewurz is one of the superstar varieties of Alsace in France. The best ooze aromas of lychee, rose, orange blossom, cinnamon, ginger, and spice. Good Gewurz will be rich and weighty, with great length of flavour.

Marsanne (*mar-SAHN*)
Clean, fresh, and fruity, this grape plays second fiddle to Viognier in France's northern Rhône Valley; however, it dominates many of the white-wine blends of the southern Rhône.

Expect ripe, peachy fruit flavours, fresh acidity, and barely a whiff of oak. With a bit of age, Marsanne takes on an amazing honeyed character and becomes slightly oilier, with more weight and richness. Outside France, you might see it in parts of Australia.

Muscat
For purposes of this book, the large Muscat family of grapes can be split into non-identical triplets: Muscat Blanc à Petits Grains, Muscat of Alexandria, and Muscat Ottonel. Wine styles vary from light, fizzy Moscato d'Asti (northwest Italy) and sweet, spirity Muscat de Beaumes-de-Venise (France's Rhône Valley) to Spain's aromatic Málagas and the unique liqueur Muscats of Australia's northeast Victoria.

Palomino Fino
(*pal-o-MEEN-o FEEN-o*)
The most important variety in the production of sherry, accounting for four of the five main styles: manzanilla,

fino, amontillado, and oloroso. Fino is the most popular and one of the greatest food wines in the world. The best are bone-dry, nutty, and slightly salty, with great mineral texture and a clean, tangy finish.

Pedro Ximénez
(*PAY-dro hee-MAY-neth*)
Although "PX", as it's more commonly called, falls into the white-grape family, this sun-loving variety produces sweet, thick, syrupy wines. Great examples are almost black in colour, viscous, and super-sweet, with intense aromas of raisin and spice.

Pinot Gris/Pinot Grigio
(*PEE-no gree/PEE-no GREE-jee-o*)
Technically, these are the same grape; the key difference lies in the style. Pinot Grigio tends to be light, delicate, and fresh, usually made in stainless-steel tanks and best drunk young, when it's zippy and vibrant. Pinot Gris is fatter and richer, with more weight and intensity, often from time spent in oak. Pinot Grigio is commonly found in the cool of northeast Italy, while Pinot Gris is never more at home than in the French region of Alsace.

Riesling (*REES-ling*)
Technically brilliant, but still a wee bit nerdy, Riesling currently represents some of this planet's great bargain wine buys. While its spiritual home is Germany, you'll find world class examples from Austria, France, and Australia. The best will have beautiful, pure, citrus fruit aromas alongside fresh-cut flowers and spice, with flavours of lemons, limes, and minerals.

Sauvignon Blanc
(*SO-vin-yon BLAHN*)
Think passion-fruit, gooseberry, elderflower, blackcurrant… even cat's pee! France, South Africa, Chile, and Australia all have a good crack at it, but New Zealand (Marlborough, to be exact) is the modern home of this variety. The best examples are pale, unmistakably pungent on the nose, painfully crisp, and ultra-refreshing with plenty of zip and racy acidity.

Sémillon (*SEM-ee-yon*)

Sémillon is native to Bordeaux in France, but it's down under in New South Wales's Hunter Valley that Semillon (note the lack of accent on the "e") has had greatest success, producing beautifully crafted and insanely long-lived wines. In its youth, great examples explode with pear, white peach, and other ripe summer fruits. But stash a bottle away for a rainy day a few years down the line, and you'll witness this variety's true magic: aromas of super-intense citrus fruit – even marmalade – alongside toast, honey, nuts, and sweet spice.

Sherry

Sherry is the English term for the wine-producing region of Jerez-de-la-Fontera in Spain's Andalucia. There are a number of styles produced in the sherry-producing triangle down there, from a number of different varieties. Wine styles can run anywhere from bone-dry to super-sweet, while the key grape varieties used to produce them are Palomino Fino, Pedro Ximénez, and Moscatel.

Verdicchio (*vehr-DIK-ee-o*)

Verdicchio is grown and produced in Italy's Marche region, making big, rich whites that are pretty neutral when it comes to aroma, but super-lemony in flavour with plenty of spice and richness. Because of its weight, it can handle oak, too, so expect to see some wooded examples.

Viognier (*vee-ON-yay*)

Viognier overflows with intoxicating aromas of apricots, orange rind, and fresh-cut flowers. It's weighty, rich, and oily in texture, with great length and beautifully soft acidity. Native to France's northern Rhône, it also shows promise in Australia and South Africa.

THE REDS

Cabernet Sauvignon
(KAB-er-nay SO-veen-yon)

King of the red grapes; the best display power, finesse, elegance, the ability to age, and universal appeal. Its home was Bordeaux, but particularly good examples now also come from Italy, Spain, Chile, Argentina, South Africa, Australia, and California. The range of flavours and aromas varies greatly, but look for blackcurrant, dark cherry, and plummy fruit alongside cedar, mint, and eucalyptus.

Carmenère *(car-meh-NAIR)*

Carmenère can be a nightmare in the vineyard: it's hard to get ripe, and once it is, you have a tiny window in which to pick it before the acidity disappears. But when it's good, it's really good! Bearing an uncanny likeness to Merlot, the best examples are bursting with super-dark fruits (plums, blackberries, and black cherries) and aromas of spice and leather.

Chianti *(ki-AN-tee)*

Chianti is a region in Tuscany made up of eight distinct subdistricts, including Colli Senesi, Classico, and Rufina. It circles the city of Florence and extends toward Sienna in the South. There are eight grape varieties permitted for use in Chianti, although few producers nowadays use all eight (some of which are white), with many preferring to focus on Tuscany's native red star, Sangiovese. Increasingly, Merlot, Cabernet Sauvignon, and Syrah are being used to "bulk up" Sangiovese's often lean and skeletal frame.

Grenache *(GRIN-ash)*

Grown widely in Spain, France, and Australia, Grenache is the workhorse of red grapes, and can be a stand-alone performer in its own right. As concentrated, weighty, fully-fledged reds (especially in France's southern Rhône), the wines sit comfortably alongside some of the world's greatest. Grenache also provides the base for many rosés:

its low tannin, acidity, and good whack of alcohol go perfect in pink.

Malbec
This red grape variety loves the sun and is found in Argentina's Andes Mountains (home to a handful of the highest-altitude vineyards on earth). These are big wines, and the best are soft and super-fruity, with plums and spice.

Merlot (*MER-low*)
Merlot has long played second fiddle to Big Brother Cabernet, often sidelined for blending. Yet it's the most widely planted red grape in Bordeaux, and in recent times, both California and Australia have developed a love affair with it. New World examples tend to be plump, with ripe, plummy fruit and naturally low tannin. Wines from north of the equator are drier, leaner, and generally less in-your-face.

Mourvèdre (*moor-VED-rah*)
The star of the southern Rhône. Along with dark, sweet fruit there's mushroom, tobacco, roast lamb – even the elephant pen at the zoo! In Spain, it's known as Monastrell and Mataro, while in Australia it goes by Mataro and Mourvèdre. Because of its funkiness, it's rarely produced as a solo variety and is usually reserved for blending.

Nebbiolo (*neb-ee-YO-lo*)
The best examples of Nebbiolo are layered and complex, oozing aromas of tar, roses, dark cherry, black olives, and rosemary. In great wines, concentrated fruit, firm acidity, and a wash of drying tannins ensure that they'll go the distance if you want to stash them away. Nebbiolo's home is Piedmont, where it stacks up to everything, from mushrooms (truffles) to chicken, rabbit, and all sorts of game right through to good old, mouldy cheeses.

Pinot Noir (*PEE-no NWAR*)
Top examples of Pinot are seductive, intriguing, even sexy, and their versatility with food is near unrivalled.

Thought of as one of the lightest reds, top examples show layers of strawberry, raspberry, plum, and dark forest fruits, with aromas of earth, spice, animal, cedar, and truffle. These wines range from delicate and minerally to silky and rich. Try those from the Côte de Nuits (Burgundy), and New Zealand's Central Otago and Martinborough regions.

Primitivo/Zinfandel

For ages we thought these were different varieties, but they're actually the same. Zinfandel ("Zin" for short) is found in the mighty USA, where most things big are seen as beautiful. In southern Italy, Primitivo rides high alongside Negroamaro and Nero d'Avola. With plenty of sweet, ripe fruit and aromas of violets and leather, this style is much more restrained than its transatlantic brother.

Rioja (ree-O-hah)

Rioja is a wine region in northern Spain best known for its rich, full-flavoured reds. Tempranillo is the star grape of Rioja, although red varieties Garnacha, Graciano, and Mazuelo are also permitted in the blend. Similarly, as a changing of the guard takes place in the region, international varieties such as Cabernet Sauvignon, Merlot, and Syrah are finding their way into Rioja's modern face with increasing frequency.

Rosé (rose-AY)

Rosé is a style of wine. It can be made sweet, dry, or anywhere in between. It can be made from just about any grape, and can come from pretty much anywhere. There are a couple of ways to make rosé. The first is to take a finished white wine and then back-blend it with some finished red. The second, and most common, way is using the *saignée* method. This is a bit like making a cup of tea, and involves leaving the skins in contact with the juice for a period of time (anywhere from a few hours to a couple of days) to get the desired level of colour, flavour, and tannin. The wine is then fermented as though it were a white wine.

Sangiovese (*san-gee-o-VAY-zay*)

Loaded with aromas of dark cherry, plum, and forest fruits, Sangiovese often also smells of tobacco, spice, and earth. Most remember its trademark "super-drying" tannins, which, without food, can make this grape a hard slog. It's native to Tuscany, where it shines as Chianti Classico and Brunello di Montalcino. More recently, it has surfaced in both Australia and the USA, but so far without the same success.

Syrah/Shiraz (*SIH-rah/SHEER-az*)

Syrah is the French name for this grape. It is lighter in body than Shiraz, with aromas of redcurrants, raspberry, plum, and nearly always white pepper and spice. Shiraz, from Australia and the New World, tends to be concentrated and ripe. At its best, it oozes plum, raspberry, earth, cedar, and freshly ground black pepper. Some New World winemakers are now calling their wines Syrah to reflect the lighter style they are now making.

Tempranillo (*tem-pra-NEE-yo*)

The grand old man of Spanish wine. Native to Rioja, it has also sunk its roots in nearby Ribera del Duero, Navarra, Priorat, and Toro. Typically, it has a solid core of dark berry fruits complete with a rustic edge that relies on savoury aromas such as tobacco, spice, leather, and earth. A recent trend has been to make international styles with big colour, big fruit, and big oak.

Touriga Nacional (*too-REE-ga nas-see-o-NAHL*)

Touriga plays a starring role in many of Portugal's great fortified wines as well as being an important component in more than a few of its new-wave table wines. Deep, densely fruited, leathery, and with an almost inky texture, Touriga needs time to mellow. Expect to smell things like dried fruit, leather, and violets, while fortified wines will be richer, stacked with dried-fruit flavour, and boasting plenty of sweetness.

The
Hot 100

Drink

Give

Dine

Splurge

Stash

As grape prices soar and good old-fashioned wine bargains climb further up the endangered species list, know that there are still plenty of great-value bottles out there to be had. Bottles that aren't difficult to find. Bottles that shouldn't set you back any more than the price of a daily travel card. As always, this chapter lifts the lid on the best 20 wines for as little money as possible. From a spread of countries, regions, varieties, and styles, these are wines for a Tuesday night in infront of the telly, wines for bringing in the weekend, wines for lazy Sunday afternoons – wines that should have you saving your travel money and walking to work instead.

20 wines for drinking now

drink

A-Mano Rosato 2007
Puglia
Italy

As the translation suggests, A-Mano is the "handmade" range of wines from Mark Shannon and Elvezia Sbalchiero's Puglian base. Applying modern technology to old-vine Primitivo that ranges between 70 and 100 years of age, these are wines that are produced thanks to no shortage of love, blood, sweat, and tears. Expect aromas of small forest berries, currants, and dried summer flowers; while in your mouth the bright, minerally texture carries plenty of sweet summer fruit, soft acidity, and a lick of dry, grippy tannin tie things up nicely. If you haven't already discovered the wines of one of southern Italy's most exciting producers, now's the time.

Yalumba Y Series Sangiovese Rosé 2007

Barossa Valley
Australia

get it for...

$$ ($10–20)

Year in year out, Yalumba's Y Series wines provide some of the best-value examples of their kind. One of the more recent additions to the Y Series family is this snappy, dry rosé made from Italy's red grape superstar, Sangiovese. A short skin contact and cool fermentation have produced a fruity, fresh style that manages to exercise restraint where many others do not. Expect a nose of raspberries, redcurrants, and spice, while in your mouth this wine has terrific balance with sweet, dark fruit and a tight, structured finish.

Coriole Redstone Shiraz / Cabernet 2005

McLaren Vale
Australia

McLaren Vale's Coriole produce some knockout wines and increasingly from non-indigenous varieties such as Sangiovese, Nebbiolo, and Fiano. As an everyday glugger, Redstone provides awesome value for money and for your 20-odd bucks you certainly get plenty of bang. From a mixture of estate-grown and brought-in fruit – a good deal of it from old vines – this is full-flavoured, peppery Shiraz propped up by a small dose of Cabernet Sauvignon. A nose full of sweet plum, leather, and spice makes way for a dark, inky mouthful of fruit and some well-judged chewy tannins.

Chapoutier Côtes-du-Rhône Villages Rasteau 2006

Southern Rhône
France

As one of the largest producers in the Rhône Valley, Michel Chapoutier has in recent years undertaken the enormous task of both converting his own vineyards and trying to convince those that he buys fruit from that organic is the way to go. No small or easy task you would imagine. From the village of Rasteau, this soft and easy-drinking red remains one of the France's great wine bargains. Assembled from the Southern Rhône trio of Grenache, Syrah, and Mourvèdre, expect flouro cherry colour with a nose of lifted raspberry, kirsch, smoke, earth, and freshly ground black pepper. In the mouth it's medium-bodied, well-fruited, and is served nicely by some dark chewy tannin.

Georges Duboeuf Beaujolais-Villages 2007

Burgundy
France

Beaujolais is the all-terrain wine style that you can definitely pair with fish, confidently drink alongside a range of spicy foods, and happily toss into the fridge without guilt. One-hundred per cent Gamay, picked from the high-altitude vineyards around the village of Chiroubles, this straightforward, light, and easy-drinking red from the self-proclaimed "King of Beaujolais" provides super-value summer sipping. Bright and explosive with zero oak influence, expect aromas of sweet cherry, violet, and musk, while in your mouth it's soft and juicy with fresh acidity and fine, slinky tannin.

Telmo Rodriguez
Al Muvedre 2007
Rueda
Spain

The Telmo Rodriguez approach is not an uncommon one: respect the past, believe in the future, do things as naturally as you can, intervene as little as possible, and let the identity of the place speak for itself via the finished product. From the tiny Valencian DO of Alicante, Al Muvedre is a down-to-earth, young, unoaked red designed to be drunk now. Aromas range from dark-berried fruits through to smoke, earth, and ground dried spice. There's good weight on the palate also, where after a wash of sweet cherry fruit a wave of fine, chewy tannins finishes things off.

Supermarket sweep

Something phenomenal has taken place in my local supermarket. Not quite an act of God, but by supermarket standards, not far off. It involves the natural food section, you know, that skinny little section sandwiched in between dried goods and gift cards – the section more commonly associated with dreadlocks, tie-dye clothes, and hand-made leather things. Well, in my supermarket that section is seriously on the shrink.

But before you start jumping up and down on your couch shouting things like "stinking hippies", "take that", and "I told you it wouldn't last", you should probably know that the natural foods section is only shrinking because it can no longer contain the sheer volume of naturally produced groceries coming onto the market, and nor can it keep up with consumer demand. Natural foods are taking over my supermarket shelves, and I reckon that's a really good thing.

Organic culture is everywhere. Once a word you simply filed in between alfalfa and yoga, organics have infiltrated all things consumable, wine included, and have quickly become a mainstream way of life. By definition, organic wines are those produced from grapes grown without the use of industrial fertilizers, herbicides, fungicides, pesticides, and excluding the addition of synthetic additives. Given our rising curiosity for knowing more about what we eat and drink, organic farming is a natural and responsible practice via which many of the world's greatest wines are produced. The growing number of great-value examples hitting the shelves is better news still.

Paxton AAA
Shiraz / Grenache 2006
McLaren Vale
Australia

The Paxton's have been growing top quality grapes in McLaren Vale for the better part of four decades during which time they've supplied fruit to some of the country's biggest names. From their own label, AAA is a classic Aussie blend from old-vine Shiraz (70 per cent) and dry-grown bush-vine Grenache (30 per cent), that forms a lush, fruit-rich red that is primed for drinking now. Expect to find a nose bursting with dark plum, pepper, and spice, while the palate is weighty and rich with plenty of bright fruit and brilliant structure. Best of all, oak has been dealt out sparingly. Elements of biodynamic practices are incorporated into vineyard management, and pretty much everything here is done by hand.

De Bortoli Gulf Station Pinot Noir 2007

Yarra Valley
Australia

BARGAIN OF THE YEAR

PRODUCER OF THE YEAR

Remembering we're not talking about a variety that's cheap to produce, De Bortoli Gulf Station Pinot Noir – sourced entirely from Yarra Valley fruit – is really exceptional value for money. With Steve Webber and Young Australian Winemaker of the Year, Bill Downie, at the controls, this is great Pinot with terrific balance and intensity. Cherry red to look at, expect a nose loaded with sweet dark fruit, earth, and sweet spices such as cinnamon, nutmeg, and clove. The palate shows great varietal definition with brilliant intensity of flavour and a wash of fine, silky tannins.

Hewitson Miss Harry GSM 2006
Barossa Valley
Australia

Dean Hewitson is an incredibly talented winemaker. He has had the good fortune of working alongside and learning from some of the best producers in the world. A liquid homage to daughter Harriet, Miss Harry is a fruit-rich blend of Grenache (55 per cent), Shiraz (33 per cent), and Mourvèdre (12 per cent) that's drawn from selected dry-grown old blocks (in most cases around 80 plus years old) in the Barossa. It also steers clear of incorporating any kind of new oak influence. Expect a voluptuous fruit-forward wine that's dense, chewy, and rich. Aromas and flavours range from sweet, dark plum and cherry fruit through to liquorice, bitter chocolate, and Christmas cake. A wave of chewy tannin balances things nicely.

Plantagenet
Omrah Shiraz 2005
Mount Barker
Australia

Plantaganet is regarded by many not just as one of Western Australia's top producers, but one of Australia's. Estate grown and produced wines are bottled under the Plantaganet label, while the "Omrah" range relies on top-quality fruit from around the state. Think sweet black cherries, wood smoke, and pepper, which just about jump all over you thanks to a small addition of Viognier. Take a slurp and find a full, seamless palate with plenty of dark fruit and great balance.

get it for...

$$ ($10–20)

Nothing fancy, just somewhere cool, dark, and vibration free. If you've got a few good bottles stashed away under the hot water service, on top of the fridge, or next to the fireplace: what are you thinking? Do the right thing and look after them properly.

Build yourself a cellar

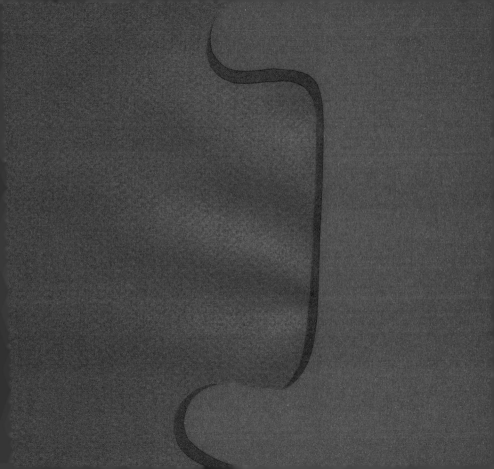

Hugel Gentil 2006
Alsace
France

get it for...

$$$ ($21–30)

Once upon a time in the fairytale-like villages of Alsace, all wines produced from a blend of noble grape varieties were labelled as "Gentil". Hugel's version continues the tradition, bringing together the noble (but slightly uncool) five-some of Gewurztraminer, Pinot Gris, Riesling, Muscat, and Sylvaner. The result is as exotic as the blend suggests, with aromas of jasmine, rose, clementine, and musk dominating the nose. The palate falls somewhere between medium- and full-bodied and, above all, is beautifully balanced.

Water Wheel Shiraz 2006
Bendigo
Australia

Water Wheel Shiraz would have to be one of the most highly awarded, heavily starred, and much scribbled about drinks this country has seen, and yet beyond all the praise it somehow remains one of Australia's foremost wine bargains. 2006 is the latest in a long line of terrific offerings from this Bendigo-based producer. Bravo. Expect to find a nose built around a core of rich, sweet plum and raspberry fruit, while aromas of milk chocolate and spice add to the equation. In the mouth the sweet fruit is backed up by fine acidity before a wash of dry grainy tannin steps in to finish things off.

Torres
Viña Esmeralda 2007
Penedès
Spain

get it for...

$$ ($10–20)

Viña Esmeralda is a dry and flamboyantly aromatic blend of Moscatel and Gewurztraminer that's been souped-up with a splash of Riesling. For a small amount of money you get a huge amount of personality in return. With zero oak influence, you can expect to find on the nose a pretty mixture of jasmine, musk, and lychee, while in your mouth this wine is crisp – nowhere near as rich as you might expect – and beautifully balanced. Just the kind of thing you would expect from Torres: one of the world's great exponents of great value drinking.

Primo Estate
La Biondina 2006
Multi-regional blend
Australia

"The young blonde" is back, and – based on what we've tasted already – she's set to be as popular as ever. From the stable of Joe Grilli, passionate supporter of all things Italian, La Biondina is a racy, drink-now mix of McLaren Vale Colombard and Adelaide Hills Sauvignon Blanc. Clean, crisp, and dry, expect a pale-gold colour followed by a ripe and rich nose of pineapple, honey, and candied citrus fruit. The palate is mineral, fresh, and lively with great concentration, stunning acidity, and terrific length of flavour.

get it for...

$$ ($10–20)

Dr Loosen "L" Riesling 2007

Mosel
Germany

With holdings throughout Germany's most famed vineyards, together with ecologically sound and sustainable practices, Ernie Loosen is widely regarded as one of finest exponents of Riesling anywhere in the world. His most basic offering is a delicate and attractive wine that walks the tightrope between sweetness and acidity with ease. Combining aromas of jasmine, mandarin, spice, and lime, it boasts a racy palate that pulls up just this side of dry. This is a stunning example from one of Germany's top producers.

get it for...
$$$ ($21–30)

Peter Lehmann
Eden Valley Riesling 2007
Eden Valley
Australia

The Eden Valley is renowned for producing a tight, steely, and firmly structured style of Riesling that has a serious capacity to age. Less fashionable than the nearby Clare Valley, good examples are readily available and remain some of Australia's great-value wine buys. Having scooped a bag of awards, this example from Peter Lehmann is right on the money. From its piercing nose of fresh lime juice and spring flowers, to its intense and angular palate, this is simply one of the year's great wine bargains.

Two of a Kind Semillon / Sauvignon Blanc 2008
Multi-regional blend
Australia

get it for...

$$ ($10–20)

While the practice of blending grapes is frowned upon in some parts of the world, particularly by those looking to capture a pure sense of place, in Australia it's about as common as putting cheese with Vegemite. From the hands of Andrew Thomas, one of the most talented young winemakers in the country, this is a cracking blend that pairs Semillon from the Hunter Valley with Sauvignon Blanc from the Adelaide Hills, and the end result is brilliant. Expect to find a compact and pure nose of lemons, apples, and pears, while laser-like acidity on the palate provides a tight, dry, and snappy finish.

Earth, wind, and fire

Imagine I told you that in order to make biodynamic wine you'd have to fill a cow's horn with manure, bury it approximately 40–60cm (15–23 in) underground in the autumn, and unearth it the following spring. You'd think I was nuts, right? Imagine I went on to tell you that the horn's contents would replace any conventional herbicides, pesticides, and fungicides that you would otherwise normally use to protect your vines against all kinds of nasty stuff, and that much of your work both in the vineyard and the winery would take place in line with the various phases of the moon – oh yeah – and naked… You'd be convinced I was either having you on, or totally off my rocker.

Rather complicated and highly controversial, biodynamic farming is the brainchild of German philosopher Rudolph Steiner.

Steiner was primarily concerned with bridging the gap between the material and the physical, and toward the end of his life, he applied his spiritual science of "anthroposophy" to agriculture.

With elements of homeopathy, astronomy, and astrology, biodynamics looks at the entire vineyard and everything in it. It's about creating a balanced and healthy eco-system, taking into consideration flora, fauna, soil fertility, and crop nutrition.

Confused? Relax, you wouldn't be alone. Even some of the biodynamic movement's biggest supporters – which include some of the world's most respected wine producers – aren't totally sure of how it works either, although all agree unanimously that their vines have never been healthier, and their wines have never tasted better.

Jim Barry Watervale Riesling 2007
Clare Valley
Australia

I've said it before, but often the best value in wine lies in lesser known countries, regions, styles, and varieties – which in the case of Australia means Riesling. And while Sauvignon Blanc and Pinot Grigio continue to get the airplay, lovers of fruity dry whites should be looking – and that's if they're not already – at this country's best white grape, Riesling. From the teeny town of Watervale in South Australia's Clare Valley comes the latest in a long line of impressive offerings from Jim Barry. Stuffed full of bright limey fruit, aromas of summer flowers, and the kind of framework that will no doubt see it last for many moons, as bargains go this wine is bound to become a perennial hit.

Giesen Sauvignon Blanc 2007

Marlborough
New Zealand

get it for...

$$ ($10–20)

Occupying the northern tip of New Zealand's South Island, Marlborough is home to one of the world's most distinctive wine styles. Love it or hate it, it's 20 years since Marlborough Sauvignon first came into our lives and it's now well and truly a household name. In fact, today, Sauvignon Blanc accounts for 78 per cent of the country's total wine exports, and, with what little land remains for planting grapes, continues to be the most planted variety in the region. This stylish example from Giesen comes from the stony soils of Rapaura within the Wairau Valley – home to many of Marlborough's finest examples of Sauvignon Blanc. A big sniff will reveal classic grapefruit, gooseberry, and mineral character, while the palate is dry, tight, and balanced beautifully by mouthwatering acidity and great length of flavour.

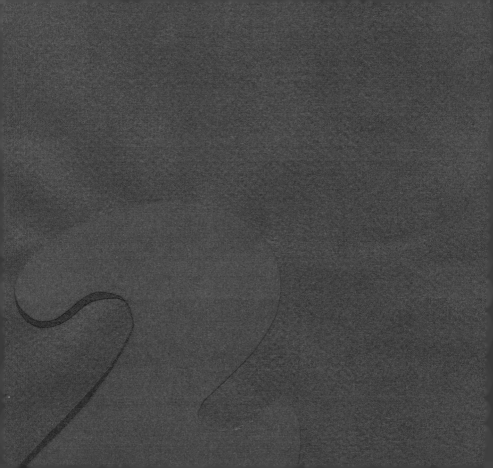

The wine section of any supermarket can be a frightening place, but it can also be the source of some great bargains – some of the best value lies in lesser known countries, varieties, regions, and styles. You might have to look a little harder to find them, but it'll be worth it.

Escape your comfort zone

T'Gallant Juliet Pinot Grigio 2008
Mornington Peninsula
Australia

get it for...

$$ ($10–20)

Pinot Grigio and Pinot Gris are the same variety: the difference in the glass comes down to climate, production, and style. In a nutshell, Grigio is the lighter, fresher expression hailing from Italy's northeast. Grapes are often picked early to maintain high levels of natural acidity while production occurs in a kind of "wham bam thank you mam" fashion to capitalize on freshness and zing. Alternatively, Pinot Gris is the French equivalent where riper fruit and a more hands-on approach to production has a tendency to produce fatter, richer examples. Juliet Pinot Grigio is a vibrant and accessible wine from the dynamic duo of Kathleen Quealy and Kevin McCarthy. A trademark nose of lemon, honeysuckle, river rock, and minerals make way for a beautifully crafted mouthful of wine that's fresh, delicate, and squeaky-clean.

You've got a new girlfriend, maybe a pay rise from the boss is on the cards, perhaps you're meeting the "in-laws to be" for the very first time, you're off to dinner with friends (who know a thing or two about wine), you forgot your dad's birthday, you need to make an apology, a bribe – perhaps it's for love, maybe its for money, it might even be for both – whatever the reason the following 20 wines are guaranteed to make even the most buttoned-up of wine connoisseurs go fuzzy. These are the 20 wines you should be giving this year.

20 wines for putting smiles on faces

give

Coldstream Hills
Chardonnay 2007
Yarra Valley
Australia

James Halliday, one of the most highly
regarded and influential members of
the international wine community,
established Coldstream Hills in
Victoria's Yarra Valley in 1985. With
Burgundy both a serious passion and
second home to Halliday, it's little
surprise that Chardonnay and Pinot
Noir – complete with European
styling – go very well here. The basic
Chardonnay is easily one of the best
of its kind on the market (being good-
value Chardonnay); complex and fine,
it sees no malolactic fermentation,
providing a crisp and mineral style
that's amply supported by rich stone
fruit. There are signs of oak on both
the nose and palate, but with only a
snip above 20 per cent new oak used
its influence is minimal.

Yarra Burn Pinot Noir / Chardonnay / Pinot Meunier Brut 2005

Yarra Valley
Australia

get it for...

$$$ ($21–30)

Established in 1975 in the foothills of Victoria's Warburton Ranges, Yarra Burn is a pioneer of Yarra Valley sparkling wine production. The first vintage of Yarra Burn sparkling was released in 1983. Nowadays, Ed Carr – perhaps the greatest sparkling winemaker outside of Champagne – is responsible not only for production, but also for the impressive haul of accolades this wine has collected over the years. Expect a compact and clean nose of tart green apples, citrus, toasted brioche, and spice, thanks to extended time on lees.In your mouth there's terrific intensity of ripe lemony fruit, a wash of fine bubbles, and a long, clean finish. Have a couple on standby.

They'll make all the difference. Avoid fancy colours, patterns, and shapes: the best glasses are clear, have a tear-drop-shaped bowl that's wider at the bottom than top, and a stem. Durability is really important, too, and while hand-made, lead-crystal glasses are lovely to drink out of, they're not necessarily the most practical for everyday use.

Buy some decent glasses

Alkoomi Frankland River Shiraz / Viognier 2007
Frankland Valley
Australia

get it for...

$$$ ($21–30)

The Frankland River sits 80km (50 miles) inland from the coast and is the coolest of all Western Australia's wine regions. It is perfectly suited to producing lean, spice-driven Shiraz, much of which is perfectly suited to a little bit of help from Viognier. And, while Shiraz/Viognier blends have grown to become a little bit like the commodores of the wine world in as much as everyone that makes wine seems to have one, Alkoomi do a very good job indeed. Here, 7 per cent Viognier was co-fermented with 93 per cent Shiraz to create a ripe and voluptuous wine that displays deep colour, spicy aromatic lift, and broad, velvety texture in the mouth. Alcohol weighs in around 13.5 per cent ABV and top-quality French oak is used sparingly.

Keep it in the closet

We don't like to talk about it, yet most blokes will agree that there's nothing quite like a week on the beach to remind you that you're not getting any younger. From the indignity of having to squeeze your love handles into last year's board shorts, to the realization that your pecks have now fully blossomed into man boobs – it's all a stark reminder that you're not what you used to be. Similarly, not all wine gets better with age, and those that do can often attribute their longevity to the grape variety/varieties used, the country and region of origin, the method of production, and how the wine was stored.

For most of us, the idea of starting a cellar is about as much a priority as starting next year's tax return. After all, aren't cellars just for the well heeled – for the really hardcore wine enthusiasts – the sacred domain of those who persist in wearing bow-ties despite the fact that they went out of fashion two decades ago? No. You don't need to know much about wine to have a cellar. And your cellar can be as basic as a simple stack of cardboard boxes in the corner of a room, or on a grander scale, cellars can be state-of-the-art, blinged-out, cavernous underground spaces.

The point is that, if you have more than just a few decent bottles lying around, then you should look after them properly, and that means finding somewhere cool, dark, vibration-free – and preferably somewhere with a lock.

Brokenwood Cricket Pitch White 2007
Hunter Valley
Australia

For more than just a few moons now, this much-loved Hunter Valley classic has been keeping thirsts quenched right around the world. As a 50/50 blend of Semillon and Sauvignon Blanc, and sourced from vineyards in both Cowra and the Hunter Valley, Cricket Pitch White is bone dry, snappy, and fresh. As you might imagine, winemaking takes place in stainless steel, which produces a clean and aromatic style of wine that displays the best character this partnership has to offer. An incredibly pure nose ranges from lifted gooseberry to blackcurrant and fresh green peas, while in your mouth it's tight and dry with razor-guided acidity cleaning things up nicely.

Innocent Bystander Rosé 2008
Yarra Valley
Australia

From a vintage that resembled Armageddon, this Yarra Valley rosé from the team (used stables just above) that is Innocent Bystander and Giant Steps is a dry, fruit-driven rosé made from Pinot Noir, assembled by winemaker Steve Flamstead. Strawberry and ripe raspberry fruit dominate the nose here, while the palate comes across as zippy, fresh, and finely structured. With its bright fresh flavours and tart drying finish, this rosé is a must for your next beachside barbeque.

Capçanes Lasendal 2005
Montsant
Spain

Home to around 70 local growers, the rejuvenated Capçanes cooperative in downtown Tarragona is today producing some very good wines indeed. And, while getting to grips with the concept of quality over quantity might have taken some growers a little longer than others, serious efforts to revert the vineyards to natural practices, to reduce yields, and improve conditions within the winery have all paid off. This example from the insanely steep terraced vineyards of Montsant is a power-packed and inky mix of old-vine organically farmed Granacha and Syrah that displays terrific weight and intensity.

McHenry Honen
3 Amigos GSM 2006
Margaret River
Australia

Having established Cape Mentelle in 1970 and the iconic Cloudy Bay in 1985, McHenry Hohnen is David Hohnen's latest venture that – together with daughter, Freya, and brother-in-law, Murray McHenry – produces a range of grape varieties and wine styles from four vineyards that employ "great grandpa farming". This is based on the idea that long before modern chemicals and synthetic additives, farmers worked to create a naturally balanced eco-system in order to get the best from their land. From the range, 3 Amigos GSM is a soft drink-now blend of Grenache, Shiraz, and Mataro, where dark fruit and lovely Rhône-like spice lead you to a palate that is plush and full of bright berry fruit.

Penley Phoenix
Cabernet Sauvignon 2006
Coonawarra
Australia

get it for...

$$ ($10–20)

In a region that's not light on stars, Penley sit happily up the sharp end of Coonawarra's distinguished heap. Its wines focus on fruit-driven, age-worthy reds that are unsurprisingly high calibre given winemaker Kym Tolley's apprenticeship under Grange master, Max Schubert – not to mention his lengthy experience at working the famed terra rossa soils of the region. Concentrated, inky, and dense, the nose of this Cabernet is loaded with aromas of cassis, leather, spice, and mint. The palate is weighty and full, with loads of fruit and brilliant structure. Best of all, the oak has been dealt out sparingly: so while this wine provides terrific drinking now, you could happily stash it under the bed for the better part of the next decade.

De Bortoli Yarra Valley Pinot Noir 2006
Yarra Valley
Australia

get it for...
$$$$ ($31–100)

PRODUCER OF THE YEAR

With Steve Webber and Bill Downie at the controls – two of Australia's most exciting winemakers – it isn't difficult to understand the buzz around De Bortoli's Yarra Valley outpost. Over the past decade all its vineyards have been re-graded according to quality, there has been a definite nod towards organic practices, vineyards have been re-orientated to reduce sun exposure, and hands have been favoured over machines. The same attitude extends to the winery where, along with stricter sorting, no cultured yeasts are used during fermentation and older oak is favoured over new. The result is lush, smooth, and elegant Pinot that any lover of top drawer Pinot Noir will appreciate.

Cullen Margaret River White 2007
Margaret River
Australia

Not only is Margaret River one of the most beautiful places on earth, but it is also home to some of the most finely tuned wines assembled anywhere in Australia. From the stables of one of this country's greatest producers comes the incredibly approachable Margaret River White: an estate-grown blend of Sauvignon Blanc, Sémillon, Chardonnay, and Verdelho. It displays a level of sophistication not often seen at this price point, which is testament to Cullen. Drinking now, expect a pretty and lifted nose of bright citrus fruit and fresh green herbs, while in your mouth the addition of a small percentage of Chardonnay is the perfect foil for the crisp and angular Sauvignon/Semillon partnership.

Bell Hill
Old Weka Pass Road
Pinot Noir 2006
Canterbury
New Zealand

Long before Bell Hill Pinot Noir got
wine-lovers around the planet frothing
at the mouth with excitement – me
included – Old Weka Pass Road
was the first example of this variety
produced by Marcel Giesen and
Sherwyn Veldhuizen at their
Canterbury estate. From a selection
of limestone-rich vineyards with high-
density planting and a mixture of
clones, this is multi-layered and purely
fruited Pinot Noir that is slightly animal,
mineral in texture, extremely seductive,
slinky, fine, and, most of all, worth
every single penny. Oak is dealt out
sparingly with the wine spending
12 months in French barrels, only
25 per cent of which are new.

Ata Rangi Crimson Pinot Noir 2007

Martinborough
New Zealand

New Zealand – the cleanest, greenest country on earth – is also one of the wine world's most diverse. And, as Syrah and Merlot go from strength to strength up north, a fragile climate and poor soils provide an excellent starting point for Pinot Noir and a cast of whites in the south. At the southern end of the North Island, Martinborough produces some of the best examples of Pinot Noir outside of Burgundy. This example from the region's top producer is ripe, plush, stylish, and jammed full of seductive fruit and spice aromas; it offers a text-book silky mouth-feel and a long, fine finish.

Archer Shiraz 2007
Heathcote
Australia

get it for...
$$$ ($21–30)

Archer Shiraz is what you end up with if you cross Heathcote's Kennedy Vintners with Australian wine-writer, show judge, consultant, former sommelier, part-time winemaker, and all-round good guy, Nick Stock. The result is delicious. This is plush, drink-now Shiraz that effortlessly ticks all the right boxes. For starters, there is a really lovely solid core of sweet, dark fruit around which you'll find aromas of meat, smoke, and Middle Eastern spice; then in your mouth Archer is full and firm with measured tannin and bright acidity.

Up and away (Part I)

"And how many bags will you be checking in today Mr Skinner?"

"Just the two," I replied.

"I'm afraid Mr Skinner any more than one will incur an additional charge of £95 (AUS$195) per bag."

Cue major jaw drop. "Why?"

But I didn't need an explanation, I knew why. This was the airline industry – the world's biggest carbon polluter – taking the initiative to offset emissions through excess baggage. Brilliant idea: I could hardly hand over my credit card fast enough.

"What do you do with the money," I asked. "Plant trees?"

"Oh no Mr Skinner, this has nothing to do with the environment – it's a baggage handlers' fee to help cover overtime. Now if you'd kindly sign here please…"

Bugger.

The planet is suffering, and while grape-growers get greener by the minute, the rest of the wine industry (which stands to feel the effects of environmental change before most) is slowly catching on. Spanish wine giant Torres is swapping over an entire fleet of company cars. "Toyota Prius for everyone," says Miguel Torres proudly – a move set to reduce the company's carbon output by around 1,000 tones per year.

Over in Oz, Yalumba have just been acknowledged by the US Environmental Protection Agency for their environmental approach to winemaking (see page 75).

It may not sound like much, but it's a start.

Henschke
Mt Edelstone 2005
Keyneton
Australia

get it for...
$$$$ ($31–100)

As the quiet achiever in the Henschke family, Mt Edelstone is a wine of phenomenal proportions. From the 40-acre vineyard of the same name, this is 100 per cent Shiraz taken from dry-grown old-vines – many of which are fast approaching 100 years of age – and yielding somewhere in the range of a tiny 2.5 tones per acre. Concentrated, inky, and dense the nose is loaded with aromas of dark plum, blackberry, pepper, liquorice, and spice. The palate is weighty, full, and saturated with sweet black fruit and spice. The oak is French, 80 per cent new, and the wine is inside it for near enough 18 months.

Stella Bella Semillon / Sauvignon Blanc 2008
Margaret River
Australia

Making its second appearance in *The Juice*, Stella Bella Semillon/Sauvignon Blanc 2008 from the hands of Western Australia-great, Janice McDonald, is yet another stylish example of this much-loved Margaret River blend – and the latest in a long line of excellent offerings from this estate. Assembled from roughly two parts Semillon for its weight, purity, and focus and one part Sauvignon Blanc for freshness, zip, and vibrancy, expect a beautifully knit, full-flavoured, long, crisp, and crunchy dry white wine perfectly geared for everyday drinking. If the sun happens to be shining in your corner of the world, then this is the wine to give.

d'Arenberg Hermit Crab Viognier / Marsanne 2006
McLaren Vale
Australia

With the Gulf of Saint Vincent a mere hop, skip, and jump away from McLaren Vale, the calcareous remains of many fossilized creatures from the deep – including the hermit crab – make up the limestone base upon which many of the region's vines are planted. Having done an about-face on the blend – Viognier and Marsanne rather than Marsanne and Viognier – Hermit Crab is full and generous with an exotic nose of apricot, orange blossom, and jasmine. In the mouth, trademark Viognier weight is underlined beautifully by Marsanne's zip and freshness, and only one-third of the blend sees time in old oak.

Kumeu River Estate Chardonnay 2006
Auckland
New Zealand

Michael Brakovich is a master when it comes to creating complex, nutty, citrus-laden examples of Chardonnay that ooze personality and style. Most impressive is the seriously detailed attention paid to this wine, given the very reasonable price tag. The Estate Chardonnay is hand-harvested, whole-bunch pressed, inoculated using wild yeasts, and a third of the wine is barrel fermented. From tightly packed and intense grapefruit character through to aromas of cashew and hazelnut, this is a lesson in just how good New World Chardonnay can be. Better still, it tastes every inch as good as it smells with focused citrus fruit, great length of flavour, and screw-capped freshness.

Which doesn't necessarily mean shelling out. If you never spend any more than £5 (AUS$10) on a bottle of wine, by spending £6 (AUS$12) – even by stretching that little further – in theory fixed production costs stay the same and what increases is the value of the liquid in the bottle, meaning the quality of what you're drinking stands to markedly improve.

Trade up

Lillydale Estate Cabernet Sauvignon / Merlot 2003
Yarra Valley
Australia

From high up in the chilly hills of Seville (that would be Seville in the Yarra Valley and not Spain), this blend of Cabernet Sauvignon (94 per cent) and Merlot (6 per cent) is the end result of an uncharacteristically warm vintage. Plush, forward, and drinking beautifully now, expect a nose filled with sweet blackcurrant, blood plum, leather, and cedar. The palate falls into the medium-bodied camp and has a lovely softness indicative of the growing conditions. Both tannin and acid are softer than usual, but well-balanced, and the wine underwent 20 months in a mixture of new and one-year-old French and American oak barrels prior to bottling and release.

Wirra Wirra Scrubby Rise Sauvignon Blanc / Semillon / Viognier 2008
McLaren Vale
Australia

The trio of Sauvignon Blanc (45 per cent), Semillon (39 per cent), and odd-man-out Viognier (16 per cent) unite here to form one of the planet's best-value dry white wines. Bizarrely, the vineyard of the same name – from which a large chunk of the Semillon component is taken – is pretty much flat and scrubless. Anyway, calling on fruit from McLaren Vale, Fleurieu Peninsula, and the chilly Adelaide Hills, a big sniff will reveal classic grapefruit, gooseberry, and mineral character, while the palate is dry, broad, and balanced beautifully by mouthwatering acidity and great length of flavour. Great for giving, but just as good for keeping.

Sutton Grange Fairbank Viognier 2007
Harcourt
Australia

Sutton Grange is located about 30km (19 miles) south of Bendigo, and borders Heathcote and Macedon. Under the supervision of Stuart Anderson (Balgownie Estate), the first vines were planted in 1998 and today include Syrah, Cabernet, Merlot, Sangiovese, Fiano, and in the case of this wine, Viognier. Viognier is a variety often guilty of carrying a few extra kilos, yet Fairbank's version made by Gilles Lapalus is a stylish, slim-line model that offers real depth and purity, minus the flab. Aromas range from apricot to white peach and orange blossom, while in your mouth this example shows terrific intensity and control.

Eat, drink, and be merry. That's what this chapter is about. This is the chapter where we lift the lid on 20 great food and wine combinations – 20 great wines that, no matter how bad you are in the kitchen, are guaranteed to bring smiles to faces. This isn't rocket science, and nor do you need to be an expert. Some of the best combinations are also some of the cheapest and easiest to reproduce. And, whether you choose to follow the rules or break them all, at the very heart of it, good food-and-wine matching knits a little bit of art with a little bit of science, and a lot of trial and error. Practice makes perfect? Bon Appetite!

20 wines to drink with food

dine

Jansz Premium Cuvée NV
Tasmania
Australia

The legendary soft-shell crab at Pacific Seafood BBQ House Restaurant (210 Toorak Road, South Yarra) arrives lightly coated in a dry batter and tossed through a mixture of garlic, sea salt, and fresh chilies. It's a tough ask for most wine, although good sparkling is an obvious choice, and the Pipers River region in Tasmania is home to some of Australia's best. Of those, the much-loved Jansz packs a bright and clean nose of green apple, citrus, bread, and honey, while in your mouth great flavour and masses of bright tiny bubbles are all you need to navigate even the trickiest of tricky textures.

Seppelt Silverband
Sparkling Shiraz NV
Great Western
Australia

get it for...

$$$$ ($31–100)

Old Kingdom (197 Smith Street, Collingwood) is a bit of an institution. It's where Melbourne goes to eat Peking Duck, via a process that starts the day before when you ring and order your duck(s), then, once you arrive, it begins. First you get a lesson in cutting the duck, then comes a lesson in assembly, and finally a lesson in folding – six o'clock to twelve o'clock etc… Just as well Old Kingdom is BYO. Produced from 100 per cent Grampians Shiraz, and with an average age of six years in the blend, Silverband Sparkling Shiraz is the latest in a long line of quality offerings from Seppelt, and manages to strike a balance between sweet and savory with ease. If Peking Duck is on your menu, have a bottle handy.

La Gitana Manzanilla NV
Jerez
Spain

get it for...

$$$ ($10–20)

The best examples of manzanilla are bone dry, slightly nutty, and have a lovely salty tang – perfect for sparking your appetite. As a result, these wines truly rise to the occasion when paired with foods such as salty green olives, fresh or jarred anchovies, caperberries, cured meats, and nuts. From the seaside town of Sanlúcar de Barrameda, this is a cracking wine that represents outstanding value for money. Pale in colour, bone dry, and with its trademark salty tang, serve cold and you'll be hard pressed to find a better food wine on the planet.

Bress Silver Chook Cabernet Rosé 2007
Harcourt
Australia

If you find yourself on the hunt for good pizza in Melbourne, make a beeline for Mr Wolf (9–15 Inkerman Street, St Kilda), where, if you're lucky, you might be offered a special like blonde pizza with calamari, smashed green olives, and spring peas, or a tried-and-tested classic such as tomato, mozzarella, olives, anchovies, capers, and chili. Whichever, a bottle of the delicious Bress Rosé to match is a must. Adam Marks produces a bone-dry style of rosé from a mixture of Cabernet Sauvignon and Cabernet Franc taken from Victoria's Harcourt Valley. Salmon in colour, expect a pretty nose of summer berries, dried flowers, and spice, while the palate is mineral and fresh with bright acidity and a clean, snappy finish.

A few things about Fairtrade and wine…

In 2003, a small community-run grape-growing/winemaking business in South Africa's Elgin Valley made history by becoming the first wine producer in the developing world to receive Faitrade accreditation. Their name, translating as "nurturing love", was Thandi.

Fairtrade came to the UK in 1992 in order to guarantee that disadvantaged producers in the developing world were getting a better deal. All Fairtrade products carry a symbol that can only be applied to products that have met criteria set out by Fairtrade standards. These standards cover things like paying prices to cover sustainable farming, paying premiums for community development, committing to partnerships that allow for long-term planning, and for sustainable production.

In 2007, just four years after Thandi received it's official accreditation, London played host to the Fairtrade wine committee's second annual wine tasting, where the number of Fairtrade-accredited wine producers – representing South Africa, Chile, and Argentina – had risen to 18. Eighteen producers who, in 2007 alone, managed to sell near enough to £8million (AUS$16.5million) – that's over 3.5 million litres (770,000 gallons) – worth of Fairtrade wine in the UK. Now that's impressive. Even more impressive is that since it's inception, sales of Fairtrade goods in the UK alone have exceeded £500million (AUS$1billion), which in turn has given around seven million people – farmers, workers, families – a shot at building a better future and the ability to compete more fairly in the global market place.

$$$ ($21–30)

S C Pannell "Pronto" 2007
McLaren Vale
Australia

You know it's been a good summer when, despite having sacrificed most of the hair on your arms and half an eyebrow to the barbeque, you managed to eat outdoors more than you ate in. The slick and affordable "Pronto" is a plush, drink now, all-terrain red from one of Australia's best winemakers, Steve Pannell. Assembled from old-vine McLaren Vale Grenache, Shiraz, and Touriga, expect plenty of sweet, dark fruit alongside a beautifully structured palate that has all you'll need to tackle even the toughest challenges the barbeque can dish up.

Donnafugata
Sedàra IGT 2006
Sicily
Italy

Char-grilled, aged rib of beef rubbed with sea salt and finished with a decent slug of peppery olive oil needs wine with muscle and structure to match. To get to the point, you need a big gutsy red, and the under-appreciated Sicilian variety Nero d'Avola – with its weight, texture, and ripeness of fruit – is right up to the job. Sedàra is a clean, modern example sourced from lofty vineyards located at 300–400m (984–1,312ft) above sea level. With only half the wine spending between six to eight months in oak, expect a bright, fruit-driven nose of sweet, dark fruit and bitter chocolate, while a soft, juicy, and well-structured mouthful of wine completes the picture.

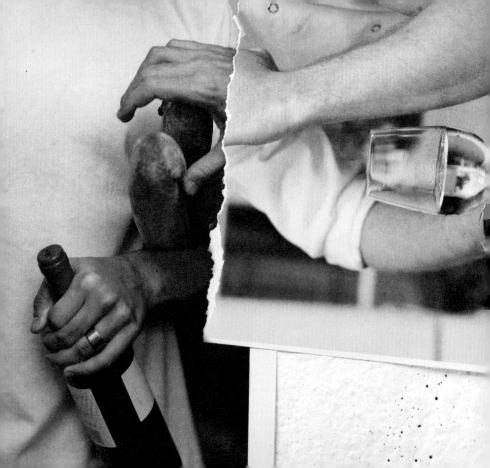

Poggiotondo Chianti Superiore DOCG 2006
Tuscany
Italy

get it for...
$$$ ($21–30)

If Friday night means pizza night in your house, then Sangiovese should be your first port of call. Aided by a small shot of Merlot, this is a quality example from the stables of renowned Tuscan consultant, Alberto Antonini. Having invested heavily in the regeneration of his family vineyards, Antonini has produced a modern style of Chianti that still manages to retain regional identity. Expect a nose of liqueur cherry, tobacco, and leather, while the not-so-typical Sangiovese palate shows off plenty of plush, ripe fruit and terrific balance between acid and tannin.

Wild Rock
Gravel Pit Red 2006
Hawke's Bay
New Zealand

For a top Merlot food match, pound together a handful of coriander seeds, cumin seeds, a pinch of dried chili, and sea salt, before rubbing liberally into a boned half leg of lamb. Chargrill each side for ten minutes on a smoking-hot barbeque, letting it rest for a further ten minutes once done. And the wine? From a patch on the famed Gimblett Gravels vineyard area – that was nearly lost to a mining company some time back – this drink-now Merlot/Malbec blend is rich with dark, sweet plums, violets, roasting meat, and spice. In your mouth it's full and firm with dry, grippy tannins and all the style you'd expect from a relative of the great Craggy Range.

Garagiste Pinot Noir 2006
Mornington Peninsula
Australia

get it for...
$$$$ ($31–100)

Along with our appetites, as the mercury rises over summer our tolerance for tannin-heavy reds all but disappears. This is a time of year for drinking and eating light. Think barbequed salmon, char-grilled tuna, pan-fried chicken, and then think Pinot Noir. Naturally light in tannin, this is beautifully structured, multi-layered, and delicious Pinot Noir from two of Australia's most promising young winemakers, Barney Flanders and David Chapman. Make no mistake, this is not top-drawer Pinot Noir that you could happily stash away, but with its sweet red fruit, exotic spice, silky mouth-feel, and focused acidity, it would be a shame not to enjoy a wine this good with food now.

get it for...

$$$ ($21–30)

Pondalowie Vineyards "MT" Tempranillo 2008
Bendigo
Australia

While many Aussie producers are still getting to grips with this Spanish native variety, Bendigo-based Pondalowie has been up and running with Tempranillo for some time now. From 100 per cent Tempranillo and with zero oak influence, expect to find aromas of sweet black cherries, aniseed, dried woody herbs, and Middle Eastern spices. On the palette it is medium-bodied with plenty of drive and grip. A combination of bright fresh fruit and a plush texture make this wine ideal for drinking now. Think garlicky Middle Eastern meatballs with couscous, parsley, mint, preserved lemon, and almonds.

Two Hands Brilliant Disguise Moscato 2008
Barossa Valley
Australia

Lemon, strawberry, pistachio, blood orange, fennel, mint – no matter what your favourite flavour of *gelati* may be, if you're after a foolproof dessert and wine combination, this is it. Light, sweet, and a little bit fizzy, the weight and sweetness of Moscato mirrors the weight and sweetness of *gelati* beautifully, while the bubbles in the wine work to clean and refresh your palate. As it involves little more than scooping *gelati* into a bowl and pulling the cork from a bottle, you have zero excuses for not having a go. This is a lovable addition to the Two Hands portfolio that already contains some of the Barossa's best wines.

Domaine de Durban Muscat de Beaumes-de-Venise 2006

Southern Rhône
France

get it for...

$$$ ($21–30)

Like most grandmas, mine was certainly no slouch when it came to making puddings. Treacle tart was nearly always top of my request list, and hers to this day is only rivalled by those served up at St John restaurant (26 St John Street, London EC1M 4AY). And, while nan may have opted for a glass of sweet sherry, Muscat de Beaumes-de-Venise is well worth a look. Domaine de Durban is home to one of the finest examples produced in the Rhône. With zero botrytis influence, this is a clean, modern style where aromas of citrus marmalade, apricot, and pineapple dominate. In your mouth expect incredible length of flavour, a little alcoholic heat, and lovely bright acidity.

Lustau San Emilio Pedro Ximénez NV
Jerez
Spain

get it for...

$$$ ($21–30)

From Jerez in Spain's south, San Emilio Pedro Ximénez – from the hands of Lustau, one of Spain's greatest producers – has an intense nose of molasses, dried raisins, spice, and spirit, while in your mouth it's syrupy, rich, and long. Serve it alongside fruit cake or sticky toffee pudding, and that's almost as good as it gets. I say almost, because there is an easier alternative. This is an absolute no brainer and your guests or better half is going to love you for it! Grab a tub of rum and raisin ice cream (vanilla is just as good), place two scoops in a bowl and liberally pour the PX over the top as though it were chocolate sauce. And there you have it: an instant classic dessert.

Giant Steps Sexton Vineyard Chardonnay 2006

Yarra Valley
Australia

A whole roast chicken in the Webber – rubbed with sea salt, cumin, and coriander seeds, stuffed with half a lemon, a knob of butter, and two half bulbs of garlic – is my idea of Chardonnay heaven. Having already scooped plenty of industry praise, this is stylish, full-flavoured Chardonnay assembled by Steve Flamstead and taken from the Sexton Vineyard, south of Healsville in Victoria's Yarra Valley. Expect to find a tightly packed nose of grapefruit, nectarine, hazelnut, and sweet spice. While in your mouth, it is pure, intense, nicely structured, and long. You might need to search a little harder than normal, but it'll definitely be worth the hunt.

Stoneleigh Marlborough Sauvignon Blanc 2008
Marlborough
New Zealand

Spring and Sauvignon Blanc go hand in hand, and Spring in the kitchen is all about new produce with freshness being the key; new peas, sweet broad beans, asparagus, and a flood of soft green herbs, and all perfectly suited to this variety. Add a squeeze of lemon, a pinch of sea salt, and a decent glug of good olive oil and you're on your way to food and wine heaven. This stylish example from the stony soils of Rapaura within the Wairau Valley – home to many of Marlborough's finest Sauvignons – would be spot on. While a big sniff will reveal classic grapefruit, gooseberry, and mineral character, the palate is dry, tight, and balanced beautifully by mouthwatering acidity and great length of flavour.

Breathing lessons

As the planet gets greener by the second, wine retailers are busy making room for a new category. That category is "carbon neutral", and it'll be coming soon to a wine aisle near you. While the rise of carbon neutral products has been inevitable given the poor health of our planet, you'll appreciate that for a winery to be 100 per cent carbon neutral – given that carbon dioxide is the by-product of fermentation – has up until recently, been very difficult indeed. With the help of carbon traders, those emissions that cannot be controlled can now be offset – a process that involves the winery being charged for the amount of trees that will need to be replanted in order to draw the same amount of carbon from the air. New Zealand's Grove Mill were the first and were quickly joined by the likes of Western Australia's Cullen, the Barossa Valley's Elderton, and South Africa's Backsburg,

Currently, the wine industry is looking at all number of ways it can save on energy and reduce the size of its carbon footprint. At ground level there is an increase in the number of energy efficient wineries, drawing on both solar and wind power, and many now include waste-water treatment plants. There are plans afoot to ship far more wine in bulk with a view to bottling closer to the point of sale, thus reducing the amount of energy used during the shipping process. Another initiative will see lighter glass and the introduction of PET plastic bottles which, all told, could reduce emissions by as much as 35 per cent. Many producers are already recycling as much as 80 per cent of their packaging.

Müller-Cartoir "MC" Riesling 2007

Pfalz
Germany

To make the classic Thai salad Som Tam, smash two cloves of garlic together with two small chilies, a few green beans, and a couple of small ripe tomatoes. Add lime juice, fish sauce, and palm sugar to taste, then two handfuls of shredded papaya and half a handful of peanuts, and there you have it. This modern, curvaceous, and just-off-dry German Riesling charged with an exotic range of aromas, including mandarin, jasmine, musk, and ginger is the ideal match for full-flavoured spicy dishes. It is a beautifully structured mouthful of wine that is pure, mineral, and low in acidity – well up for the challenge of Som Tam.

Evans & Tate Margaret River Dry White 2007

Margaret River
Australia

My salad of last summer was char-grilled prawns, cucumber, mango, shallots, coriander, mint, and lime juice, and nine times out of ten E&T's Margaret River Dry White was the wine match. Evans & Tate, now under the ownership of McWilliams, have long been one of Australia's much-loved brands, and home to a range of wines that has always offered great value for money. Assembled from a lean and racy equal-parts mix of Sauvignon Blanc and Semillon, expect an explosive nose of bright tropical fruit and fresh summer herbs. In your mouth it is clean, crisp, bone dry, and dangerously easy to swallow.

Charmers Vermentino 2006
Mildura
Australia

get it for...

$$$ ($21–30)

Vermentino is a late-ripening white grape variety, which, while widely grown throughout Italy, has its origins in Spain, Madeira, and Portugal. In more recent times it has popped up in Australian vineyards, and largely thanks to cuttings propagated in Bruce Charmers mind-boggling nursery on the outskirts of Mildura. From the newly established Charmers range of wines, this is crisp, racy, dry Vermentino that just so happens to be as good with food as it is at quenching thirsts. Expect a nose full of green apples, pears, and almonds, while in your mouth it's restrained, lemony, and superbly balanced.

And by that I don't mean burying your head in a stack of wine books (though it's worth having a few). Just go out and find yourself a good food and wine magazine, a decent wine website, or the regular wine column in your favourite paper and read. Every writer has a different style just as they have different tastes in wine. Find out what works for you.

Do a bit of reading...

Primo Estate Joseph Botrytis Riesling / Traminer "La Magia" 2006

Adelaide Plains
Australia

"La Magia" (the magic) is a botrytis-style Riesling from Primo Estate's Joe Grilli. Fruit is drawn from a mixture of sources and includes 62 per cent Eden Valley Riesling for structure, 23 per cent Clare Valley Riesling for the classic Riesling spectrum of flavour, and finally 15 per cent Coonawarra Traminer for aromatic lift. The result is astonishing. Citrus marmalade, quince, blossom, and sweet spice hum away on the nose. In your mouth you get amazing concentration of flavour that's lifted beautifully by focused acidity. If you're a lover of cheese, then a slab of Gorgonzola dolce, a couple of ripe figs, and a drizzle of good honey will be all you'll need to get you seeing stars.

Escarpment Pinot Gris 2007
Martinborough
New Zealand

Twenty-five years ago, Martinborough became the world's first scientifically researched wine region. The science worked: today, it is home to some of the most sought-after examples of Pinot Noir outside Burgundy, and it has also done well with a handful of other varieties. From the air, Martinborough's vineyards almost look as though they've crawled out of the river and are slowly over-running the town. Pinot Gris is a perfect illustration of how good the "other varieties" can be. Expect aromas of tropical fruit and fresh flowers followed by a softly textured and rich palate, with good length of flavour and low-level natural acidity.

Although wine today is a very different beast to wine 20 years ago, not every bottle of wine on the shelf is designed to drink well within seconds of you leaving the supermarket. Some bottles will need time to gather dust before really showing their best, and getting hold of them shouldn't cost you a fortune, or even require you to own a fancy cellar. Wine is an amazing drink, and some of it is made all the more amazing by time. So, go on, make patience your virtue this year, as these are the 20 wines well worth waiting for.

20 wines to blow the rent on

splurge

Billecart-Salmon Brut Rosé NV

Champagne
France

If love is in the air in your neck of the woods, then this cracking rosé from one of Champagne's much-loved stars is an essential splurge. Assembled from 40 per cent Chardonnay, 20 per cent Pinot Meunier, and 40 per cent Pinot Noir – eight per cent of which is made into a still red wine and then back blended into the finished product – "Billy" rosé is little short of love in a glass. From its salmon pink tone and delicate nose of ripe Pinot fruit, summer flowers, and spice through to its pure and tightly structured palate, this wine consistently rates as my favourite rosé Champagne and is chock full of style and grace.

Egly-Ouriet
Blanc de Noirs NV
Champagne
France

get it for...

$$$$$ ($100+)

The Egly family are something of an anomaly in Champagne. For starters they are a small family-owned and run operation. They also happen to own many of their own vineyards, giving them greater control over their fruit source. To that end the Eglys also buck the trend of using any kind of chemical herbicides, pesticides, or fungicides by choosing to employ the skills of Claude Bourguignon – one of the world's foremost soil experts. Drawn from vineyards ranging from 30 to 50 years of age, and bottled with zero *dosage* (a sweetened base wine), expect a rich, leesy nose crammed with intense Pinot fruit and spice. The palate is precise, dry, beautifully structured, and built for special occasions.

Reality bites

Boot Camp, *Wife Swap*, *Big Brother* - I've got a reality TV idea for you. It's called "Pick a Winner", and, while the title needs work, it involves taking anyone who thinks tasting wine for a living sounds easy and subjecting them to a week in the life of a wine judge – their aim to pick the best wines from thousands.

Day one will see our contestants taste and write notes on 100 or so wines in the morning, then struggle through a further 100 after lunch. We'll be amazed as they finish the day with a couple of cold beers, we'll cringe as they chat and forget their teeth are stained purple, laugh when they fall asleep on the train, and cry as they have to get up and do it all again the next morning. For many seasoned campaigners of the International Wine Show circuit, this is all in a day's work.

While wine judging may well be a skill in itself, you should be aware that not all wine shows are held in equal regard, and as consumers, you need to be really careful when blindly buying bottles of wine plastered with gold stickers for this very reason. If you don't know a huge amount about wine, then it's very easy to be lead by aesthetics. A pretty label is a great way to sell an ordinary bottle of wine, while back labels will never tell you "how bad a wine is". It's really important to remember that the reputation of the producer whose name appears on the label counts for everything.

Roger Sabon Châteauneuf du Pape "Le Secret des Sabon" 2005

Southern Rhône
France

From a domain that has been called "the reference point for Châteauneuf du Pape" on more than one occasion, "Le Secret des Sabon" is a very special and – at less than 200 cases per year – very limited cuvée taken from 100-year-old vines planted by the grandfather of current owner Jean-Jacques Sabon. While production methods remain a closely guarded secret, this is a wine of epic proportions and concentrated, inky, plush, and dense fruit is what you should brace yourself for. As dark sun-drenched flavours, dried woody herbs, liquorice, and spice flood your nose, a mouthful will unleash a wave of ripe, sweet, dark plum and macerated cherry, nicely knit oak, and balanced dry grippy tannins to finish.

Viñedos Orgánicos Emiliana Coyam 2006
Colchagua
Chile

get it for...

$$$ ($31–100)

Alvaro Espinoza is not your average Chilean winemaker. Having all but single-handedly pioneered organic and environmentally responsible viticulture in South America during the mid-nineties, Espinoza has now trained his sights on converting all of his 593 acres of vineyards (spread across Colchagua, Maipo, and Casablanca) to biodynamics. One of the resulting wines, "Coyam" is a lush, expressive mix of low-yielding Cabernet Sauvignon, Merlot, Carmenère, Syrah, and Mourvèdre. It spends near enough 12 months in French oak and is bottled without fining or filtration. This is terrific wine: polished and pure, with a serious core of dark fruit, chocolate, leather, and spice. The palate is sweet, dense, and inky, with fresh acidity and fine, drying tannin.

Escarpment "Kupe" Pinot Noir 2006
Martinborough
New Zealand

Larry McKenna's quest to produce top-drawer Pinot Noir from his Escarpment project has been duly rewarded with the third release of "Kupe" – a snapshot of the close-planted Te Muna Road vineyard in Martinborough. Concentrated, perfumed, and with more than a glancing nod towards Burgundy, the '06 model displays a tightly wound core of dark, sweet fruit underpinned by hints of earth, spice, and deftly handled cedary oak – 50 per cent of which is new. Weighing in at 14.1 per cent ABV, the palate is generous, silky, and long and is testament to McKenna's skill with this difficult child of grape varieties.

Craiglee Shiraz 2005
Sunbury
Australia

Craiglee is a leisurely two-café-lattes' drive northwest of Melbourne. As one of Victoria's first vineyards, today, under current owner Pat Carmody, it remains a benchmark within the Australian wine community. Included in the coveted Langton's *Classification of Australian Wine* and a regular darling of the wine press, Craiglee's spicy, cool-climate Shiraz is simply one of the finest examples of its kind produced in the Southern Hemisphere. 2005 was a textbook vintage, and the wines have Craiglee's typical nose of blood plum, liqueur cherry, and ground black pepper. The palate is spicy and seamless with a firm and balanced structure that ensures this wine has a long future.

Mt Difficulty
Pinot Noir 2007
Central Otago
New Zealand

get it for...

$$$$ ($31–100)

With a landscape that resembles the moon, a limited water supply, and the kind of fragile climate that should see grape-growing classified as an extreme sport, Central Otago is unique in the world of wine production. It also has a habit of producing some of the most exciting examples of Pinot Noir outside of Burgundy. Mt Difficulty has been at it since 1992, with winemaker Matt Dicey at the helm since 1998. In this wine, fermentation was warm and fast and included close to 20 per cent whole bunches. Vivid red, expect a nose of liqueur cherry, violet, smoke, and spice, while in your mouth a silky texture and super-fine tannin frame channel incredible fruit intensity.

Bouchard Père & Fils Volnay "Clos des Chênes" 2005

Burgundy
France

get it for...
$$$$$ ($100+)

2005 was a dreamy vintage in Burgundy. For starters, a mild, sunny growing season ensured that what was hanging on the vine at harvest time was top drawer. The resulting wines are stunners. From the teeny tiny chalk/clay-based "Clos des Chênes" vineyard – which at 2.1 acres produces little more than 4,000 bottles per year – expect to meet a wave of ripe raspberry and cherry Pinot fruit, while in the mouth there is huge intensity, velvet-like texture, and fine structure. There is real depth and richness here, but not at the expense of the acidity and grip that defines this vintage's top wines. Also, when it comes to doing your shopping, just be sure you're buying the right Bouchard, as there are others!

Kooyong Ferrous Pinot Noir 2006
Mornington Peninsula
Australia

While the Kooyong range of single-vineyard Pinot Noirs are all worth swapping your vitals for, it's wine from the Ferrous vineyard that gets my heart racing. Where "Meres" is pretty and delicate, and "Haven" dark and brooding, "Ferrous" manages to land somewhere smack in the middle, striking the perfect balance between power and finesse, and adding a little magic of its own. As you can imagine, pretty much everything on this estate is done by hand, and those lucky enough to get their hands on a bottle can expect a multi-layered wine that is incredibly pure, slightly animal, beautifully textured, sparingly oaked, seductive, slinky, fine, and long.

get it for...

$$$$ ($31–100)

Paul Jaboulet Aîné
Hermitage La Chapelle 2005
Northern Rhône
France

Sold to the Frey family (owners of Château La Lagune in Bordeaux) in 2005, there has been a real return to form at Jaboulet in recent times. With styles produced both north and south of Lyon, the undoubted jewel in the Jaboulet crown is the prestigious La Chapelle from Hermitage in the North. One-hundred per cent Syrah and a blend of selected plots from within the La Chapelle vineyard, expect a deep and pure wine sporting a nose of bright cherry, plum, forest fruit, meat, smoke, and spice. There is excellent weight in the mouth, too, with nicely knit oak – none of which is new – followed closely by bright acidity and a wash of firm grainy tannin.

Domaine Leflaive Puligny-Montrachet 2007
Burgundy
France

In 1990, Anne-Claude Leflaive famously served her British distributors two glasses of the same wine asking which they preferred – one had been produced organically, the other biodynamically. Without knowing how either had been made, there was unanimous support in the group for wine two. What Anne-Claude Leflaive already knew, they had confirmed, and by the following year she had moved her entire production to biodynamics. With Pierre Morey behind the winemaking controls, this Puligny emerges with a piercing nose of crème brûlée, cashew, grapefruit, nectarine, and pork rind. In your mouth it is rich and intense with bright mineral texture, serious length, and the kind of structure that will see it shine for many moons yet.

Arrivo Nebbiolo 2006
Adelaide Hills
Australia

get it for...
$$$$ ($31–100)

Armed with a global perspective and a wealth of industry experience, Sally McGill and Peter Godden set about looking for the perfect spot to cultivate and produce Nebbiolo in Australia. They settled on the Adelaide Hills and quickly went about gathering a range of clone material to trial. The first release, which was greeted by widespread acclaim, came in 2004. Aided by an extra long 72-day maceration, the 2006 model steps up the pace. Expect a nose layered with morello cherry, rose petal, black olive, rosemary, tobacco, and exotic spice, while in your mouth Arrivo is intense yet delicately textured, beautifully balanced, and above all else, extremely seductive.

Grattamacco Bolgheri Superiore DOC 2005
Tuscany
Italy

Established in the early eighties by one-time wine retailer Piermario Cavallari, Grattamacco continues to produce – in an almost "blink and you'll miss it" kind of way – terrific wines minus the hype generated around those of his fellow neighbours. Assembled from a typical blend of Cabernet Sauvignon, Merlot, and Sangiovese – that changes by way of percentage depending on the vintage – expect a dense core of dark morello cherry surrounded by aromas of fresh tobacco, leather, and dried spices. In the mouth it is mineral, rich, and rounded by a wash of trademark grippy Sangiovese tannin.

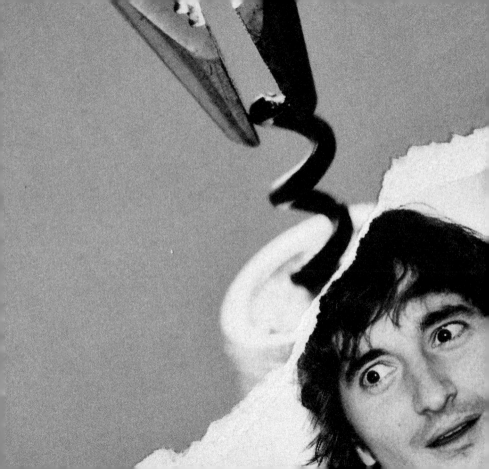

Henriques & Henriques 10-year-old Malmsey Madeira NV

Madeira
Portugal

Madeira is a unique style of fortified wine from the volcanic island of the same name that, because of heat and oxygen exposure during production, possesses distinctive character. Each wine is usually made from one of four different varieties, Sercial, Verdelho, Bual, or Malmsey, which vary in style from dry to sweet in the above order. Age plays a big role in determining end quality. Produced entirely from the Malmsey variety, this wine – which has been aged in cask for 10 years prior to being bottled – is copper/mahogany in colour and smells of dried fruit, exotic spice, and spirit. In the mouth it is sweet, nutty, and beautifully textured – still with very fresh acidity and a long, clean finish.

Giaconda Nantua
Les Deux 2007
Beechworth (Victoria)
Australia

Giaconda is now something
of a legend. Not only does Rick
Kinzbrunner's Chardonnay rank among
the world's best, but it is arguably
Australia's finest. In 2001, Kinzbrunner
added two new lines to his portfolio:
"Aeolia", a 100 per cent Roussanne
given the same Rolls Royce treatment
as his prized Chardonnay, and
"Nantua Les Deux", a delicious
blend of Chardonnay and Roussanne
that offers serious value for money.
Grapefruit and nectarine-like fruit take
centre stage alongside aromas of fresh
toast, grilled hazelnut, and pork rind.
The palate is long, rich, minerally, and
lush. A worthy and welcome addition
to the Giaconda stable.

Water into wine

You know that we're talking about a precious commodity when at up to £1 (AUS$2) a bottle, a single litre of water is often more expensive than a single litre of petrol.

Water is one of the most important ingredients in wine production. Without water, you simply cannot make wine. The irony is that while the wine industry stands to feel the effects of climate change long before most, it also happens to be one of agriculture's biggest water users.

To give you an idea just how big that is, to make a single litre of wine in Australia takes near enough to seven litres of water. And that's just to make the wine. To grow the grapes that eventually make that single litre of wine takes closer to 400 litres of water. In case you are still reeling from that figure – that

was around 400 litres of water on average just to make a single litre of wine. As a result, water-saving initiatives are fast becoming both mandatory and commonplace within the Australian wine industry.

Many of Australia's biggest wine producers have already developed and installed their own waste-water treatment plants allowing them to re-use reclaimed water from their wineries to irrigate their vineyards. Other initiatives include the use of various mulches in the vineyards in order to minimize the amount of evaporation from the soil, and employing the use of soil monitors to regulate irrigation throughout the vineyards, irrigating only when needed and only at night in order to reduce evaporation.

It might not sound like much, but it's a start.

S·JOSEP

Pierre Morey Meursault 2005

Burgundy
France

As winemaker for the iconic Domaine Leflaive since 1995, Pierre Morey knows a thing or two about producing complex, multi-tiered, and age-worthy examples of Chardonnay. As at Domaine Leflaive, biodynamic practices (employed since 1997) play a huge role in Morey's own vineyards – 22.2 acres in total, spread across holdings in Meursault, Monthélie, Pommard, and Puligny-Montrachet. From a brilliant year for white wine in Burgundy, this is stylish, full-flavoured Chardonnay crammed with aromas of grapefruit, nectarine, hazelnut, and sweet spice. The palate is pure, mineral, racy, and wound-up tightly with plenty to offer underneath. In a word, awesome!

Highbank Coonawarra 2003
Coonawarra
Australia

Dennis Vice has long championed the benefits of organic viticulture, and this wine – with considerable age already under it's belt – comes from the tiny, organic, Vice family vineyard on Coonawarra's famed terra rossa soil. Basket-pressing and a decent stint in fine-grained French oak has produced a nose with a confit of dark fruit, leather, and cedar, while the palate is lush and seamless with real weight and intensity. That power is matched beautifully by soft acidity and a wave of firm, drying tannin. Stick it away for a while or decant and enjoy now.

Planeta Cometa 2007
Sicily
Italy

get it for...
$$$$ ($31–100)

As the wines of southern Italy continue to win hearts the world over, Sicily's star producer, Planeta, remains the measuring stick for quality and success. This is the estate that, through serious attention in the vineyard and a real focus on both international and indigenous varieties, has really helped to put Sicily on the wine map. The latest offering of the flagship white, Cometa, is a mighty example of Fiano di Avellino (one of Campania's five appellations), which bears considerable elegance and restraint for a wine of its size. Expect grapefruit, white peach, and fennel on the nose, while in your mouth it's rich, spicy, and structured beautifully with gentle acidity and flavour that seems to hang around forever.

Tscharke Only Son Tempranillo 2004
Barossa Valley
Australia

get it for...

$$$ ($21–30)

European by name, Barossa by nature, Damien Tscharke's wines have racked up considerable and deserved praise since first hitting the market back in 2006. From an initial desire to explore how and what alternative varietals could work in the Barossa, Tscharke – who is hands-on from start to finish – now produces a range of wines under his own label that includes Albariño, Tempranillo, Graciano, Zinfandel, and Montepulciano. His Tempranillo, which includes a small percentage of Graciano, is like a caged animal – from its tightly wound nose of plum, liquorice, leather, cocoa, and spice to its rich and full palate rammed with dark fruit, fresh acidity, and finely tuned tannin.

Clonakilla Viognier 2007
New South Wales
Australia

get it for...
$$$$ ($31–100)

John and Tim Kirk are the father-and-son team behind Clonakilla, one of Australia's leading boutique producers. Apart from crafting one of Australia's finest cool-climate examples of Shiraz, they also produce very good Viognier. This is a cracking example with all the aromatic flamboyance you'd expect from this variety, yet without the flabby, alcoholic palate that holds so many other examples back. Expect a nose full of ripe apricot, orange rind, and fresh-cut flowers, while the palate displays slippery texture and good intensity. Low-level natural acidity keeps things framed nicely.

Find a decent wine shop and get to know the guys behind the counter. Tell them what type of wine you like drinking and get them to offer some recommendations. The more specific you can be about what you do or don't like, the better your chances are of ending up with a decent bottle. And, most importantly, try as many different wines as you can.

Make some new friends

Although wine today is a very different beast to wine 20 years ago, not every bottle of wine on the shelf is designed to drink well within seconds of you leaving the supermarket. Some bottles will need time to gather dust before really showing their best and getting hold of them shouldn't cost you a fortune, or even require you to own a fancy cellar. Wine is an amazing drink, and some of it is made all the more amazing by time. So, go on, make patience your virtue this year, as these are the 20 wines well worth waiting for.

20 wines for drinking later

stash

Delamotte Brut Blanc de Blancs NV
Champagne
France

Research (and lots of counting) tells us there are around 250 million bubbles in every bottle of Champagne. Of course, not all bubbles are the same size, and much depends on where the wine is from and how much love it gets during production. The talented team at Delamotte (sister winery of Salon) give this wine – from 100 per cent Chardonnay – a whole lot of love. Four years in the cellars prior to shipping also help make it one of the best-value examples of Blanc de Blancs Champagne on the market. Expect aromas of toast, citrus, honey, and spice coupled with masses of fine, persistent bubbles – possibly 250 million of them – great length of flavour and a long, tight finish.

Fonseca Vintage Port 2003
Douro
Portugal

get it for...
$$$$$ ($100+)

Designed to make you wait, vintage port does its ageing in bottle and often needs a couple of decades (seriously) to unwind. With time, these wines reveal a deep and complex nose of dark spiced fruits, bitter chocolate, and nicely worn leather. What often starts out tasting harsh and extractive in its youth, usually blossoms into a plush, bittersweet, and delicious mouthful of wine with age. Fonseca has produced many of the region's finest ports since the eighteenth century, and continues today as the measuring stick of quality for many others. Hold until 2020 – if you can bear it!

Taylors Clare Valley Riesling 2008

Clare Valley
Australia

get it for...

$$ ($10–20)

With last year's offering having scooped a bag of prizes, including a gold medal at the 2007 Royal Perth Show, the latest offering from Clare-based Taylors looks to be par for the course. Apart from their very reasonable price point, these wines remain incredibly popular, due in part to the fact that Taylors manage to stuff a huge amount of content into this wine's skeletal Clare framework. Hot off the press, the 2008 version is packed with pure lemon and lime citrus, spice, and biscuit notes, while in the mouth the wine shows a lovely combination of sweet and sour with rich limey fruit, tangy acidity, and a bone-dry finish.

Tyrrell's Lost Block Semillon 2007

Hunter Valley
Australia

It's enough to make you blush: that a wine that offers so much on the surface, and beyond – iconic Aussie variety from iconic Aussie producer – can end up costing so little. Still, I'm not complaining, with bargains in the wine world all but an endangered species, this is a ripper. The Hunter has a knack for turning out nervy young examples of Semillon that, like this wine, come across straw-green in colour and literally explode in your face with aromas of lemon sherbet, green apple, and summer herbs. The palate is bright, fresh, and packed with zip and zing. Stash it five, even ten years, and it will turn into a wine of mega-proportions: vastly different, honeyed, and endlessly complex.

McWilliams Mount Pleasant Elizabeth Semillon 2003
Hunter Valley
Australia

Hunter Semillon is one of the most iconic wine styles produced in Australia (*see also* previous wine). The best examples display an effortless ability to age – often outliving those that put them together. Cellared for four years prior to release, Elizabeth 2003 remains a pup, and, provided you look after it, should comfortably cruise well into middle age (7–10 years). Currently you can expect to find a tightly wound wine where lemons, tart green apples, and bees wax all make an appearance on the nose. In your mouth, the palate is similarly tight and firm. Given time, this wine will unwind to reveal a richly fruited core of citrus marmalade, honeyed toast, and spice.

Pizzini Nebbiolo 2003
King Valley
Australia

get it for...
$$$$ ($31–100)

It's fair to say Joel Pizzini's winemaking debut raised more than just a few eyebrows. Sporting everything you'd expect to find from classic and far pricier examples, Pizzini Nebbiolo 2002 – "Wine of the Show" at the Australian Alternative Varieties Wine Show 2007 – was, well, an absolute showstopper. Carrying on in the same fashion, but from a year that dealt out considerably warmer conditions, the 2003 is an equally sleek and stylish drink. Aromas range from tar to roses to black olives and sweet dark cherry fruit, while in your mouth it's mineral, intense, fine, and framed by a wash of light, fine tannin.

Robinvale Wines Kerner 2002
Orange
Australia

Kerner is what you get when you cross Riesling and Trollinger, and while there is literally only a sprinkling of it left anywhere, the biodynamic Robinvale Wines in the Murray Darling Basin is one producer that happens to do it very well. Take, for example, the age-defying 2002 that, with six years under its belt, still looks as fresh as a daisy. Bright gold-green in appearance, the nose is rich and explosive, with grapefruit, lime zest, spice, and mineral characters all vying for attention. The palate is rich, taught, and intense, with stunning acidity and incredible length of flavour.

Quartz Reef
Pinot Noir 2007
Central Otago
New Zealand

get it for...

$$$$ ($31–100)

Over time, Martinborough has set the pace for New Zealand Pinot Noir, but a rise in the number of staggeringly good wines from Central Otago (and, more recently, Marlborough) has really put a cat among the pigeons. And, while Central Otago might not have vine age on its side, it does have a dreamy mix of clones together with unique microclimates perfectly suited to producing great Pinot Noir. Rudi Bauer's Quartz Reef ranks among the region's finest. To see it at its best, hold on until 2010.

Livered

All my mates are detoxing. "Need to give our livers a chance to do what they're made for," says one. Whatever. Given that I taste wine for a living, the concept of detox isn't one that sits all that comfortably with me. I momentarily think about going in to bat for wine and its many health benefits, before realizing that in the case of more than just a few of my mates, wine probably isn't the main offender. There are very few days in my life when I do not drink. It's my job, and besides, I enjoy a couple of glasses of wine with my dinner. Although in saying that, rarely do I drink more than that during the week, and if I do get drunk, it's never on wine.

There was a time not so long ago when wine was seen as the medical world's great hope. The combination of alcohol and acidity proved to be a winning combination in tackling all manner of injury and illness and its healing properties were praised and prescribed by doctors right around the globe. But with the latter part of the twentieth century came advances in medicine and technology, not to mention different ways of thinking. For the first time the healing properties of wine were scrutinized and Prohibition in the US censored any mention of alcohol, wine included.

Today, with modern thinking, further medical advances, and interest in subjects such as the French Paradox, most experts would argue that the majority of healthy people who drink wine regularly and in moderation remain healthy.

Bottoms up!

De Bortoli Noble One 2005
Griffith
Australia

PRODUCER OF THE YEAR

Cheese fans take note: the next time you're offered a glass of port to go with your Stilton, politely decline and order yourself a glass of Australia's most famous sweet wine instead. Having won a swag of trophies, Noble One was born in 1982 via a bold and deliberate attempt to create a sweet wine from botrytis affected grapes. It remains one of Australia's most highly awarded and sought after wines. Expect a nose overflowing with ripe stone fruit, sweet orange marmalade, and spice, while the palate is bright and full – not cloying – with a long, crisp finish.

William Fèvre
Petit Chablis 2006
Burgundy
France

get it for...

$$$$ ($31–100)

Classically styled and beautifully made, this is pristine Chablis from one of the region's brightest stars. As some of the most pure expressions of Chardonnay you can find, wines from the Fèvre stable tend towards being squeaky clean, mineral in texture, and often void of oak influence. Aromas and flavours range from lemon and honey through hay to chalk. Taken from the Chablis sub-district of Petit Chablis, this fine example from the highly regarded 2006 vintage is certainly no exception. Stick some away for the better part of the next decade.

Sorrenberg Chardonnay 2006
Beechworth
Australia

Barry Morey is a great winemaker, a passionate exponent of biodynamics, and a really good bloke. The Chardonnay from his Beechworth estate has plenty of fans, and is included in Langton's Classification of Australia's top 101 producers. The 2006 Chardonnay is right up to scratch, a labour-intensive production including indigenous yeast fermentation, 100 per cent malolactic fermentation, 12 months on lees with regular stirring, and finally, eight months in French oak – 25 per cent of which is new. The resulting wine shows plenty of slick citrus/stone fruit on the nose together with my mum's Anzac biscuit mixture, and restrained nutty oak. The palate unwinds with mineral precision, carries amazing length of flavour, and seems to go on forever.

Shadowfax Chardonnay 2006
Yarra Valley
Australia

get it for...

$$$ ($21–30)

A whole roast chicken in the Webber, rubbed with sea salt and fennel seeds, and stuffed with half a lemon, a knob of butter, and two halved bulbs of garlic, is a heavenly accompaniment to this wine. Having already scooped a bag of awards, Yarra Valley's Shadowfax Chardonnay – assembled by Matt Harrop and drawn from vineyards in Geelong, Macedon, Beechworth, and the Cardinia Ranges – is stylish and full-flavoured. Expect to find a tightly packed nose of grapefruit, nectarine, hazelnut, and sweet spices. In your mouth the palate is pure, intense, nicely structured, and long. You might need to search a little harder than normal to find this wine, but it'll be worth the hunt.

Cape Mentelle Trinders Cabernet Sauvignon / Merlot 2006

Margaret River
Australia

We all have things that make us feel at home: a favourite armchair, an old photo, a good book, a well-worn pair of Moccies… One of mine is Trinders – a wine that's been making me feel at home for just about as long as I've been working in wine. Trinders is a Bordeaux-style blend of Cabernet Sauvignon, Merlot, Cabernet Franc, and Petit Verdot that is sourced from both the Trinders and Foxcliffe vineyards in Margaret River. Expect a sweet and dusty nose of blackcurrant, smoke, and leather, while the palate is similarly concentrated with Merlot helping to soften, round, and fill in the blanks of an already sleek and stylish Cabernet framework.

Dry River Pinot Noir 2006
Martinborough
New Zealand

Dr Neil McCallum established the initial eight-acre Dry River Vineyard on the Martinborough terrace in 1979. Today, Dry River's vineyard holdings account for 30 acres spread over three vineyards (Dry River, Craighall, and Lovat), and include plantings of Riesling, Gewurztraminer, Sauvignon Blanc, Chardonnay, Pinot Gris, Viognier, Merlot, Syrah, and last but not least, Pinot Noir. From the 2006 vintage, this is robust Pinot Noir that displays plenty of personality and charm. A concentrated nose of dried fruit, spice, and game makes room for a solid and delicious mouthful of wine that is sweet, pure, and underlined by its fine silky texture. Acidity is bright and tannins are delicate, round, and supportive.

Tahbilk Marsanne 2006
Nagambie Lakes (Victoria)
Australia

get it for...

$$$$ ($10–20)

Sporting a string of accolades that would make most competitors blush, Tahbilk Marsanne is one quiet achieving Aussie wine that consistently overdelivers considering its price tag. With fruit harvested from plantings dating back to 1927, here's a wine that – while drinking beautifully right this second – will hit its teens developing into a complex and honeyed wine. Packing green apple, pear, honeysuckle, and plenty of citrus zip and zing, the welcome addition of a screwcap since the release of the 2005 vintage is great news and should see these already long-lived wines long outlive most of us!

Pyramid Valley Lebecca Vineyard Riesling 2005
Canterbury
New Zealand

get it for...

$$$$ ($31–100)

Mouthwatering wine from one of the most exciting producers in New Zealand. Mike Weersing studied winemaking in Burgundy, and has also worked for some of the planet's finest producers. In his Canterbury-based Pyramid Valley vineyards he incorporates biodynamic principles wherever possible to produce wines like this knockout Germanic-styled Lebecca Riesling. Sweetness, acidity, and alcohol are perfectly tuned to give a terrific proposition for your cellar. Expect aromas of pretty jasmine flowers, mandarin, and Golden Delicious apples that make way for a delicate mouthful of wine that's off-dry and balanced beautifully by mineral texture and super fresh acidity.

Isole e Olena
Cepparello 2003
Tuscany
Italy

WINE OF THE YEAR

After the disappointingly wet 2002, the abnormally hot 2003 brought about further frustrations to many Italian growers – particularly those in Tuscany. From a year that produced a raft of over-ripe and unbalanced wines, Paolo de Marchi's flagship wine, Cepparello, is both an exception and a serious show-stopper. Assembled from 100 per cent Sangiovese, this multi-layered wine packs a dense core of dark morello cherry fruit surrounded by aromas of fresh tobacco, liquorice, leather, dried spice, and deftly used French oak – one third of which is new. For such a warm vintage there is real elegance on the palate, too, with a bright mineral texture and a terrific intensity of fruit. It winds up with a wash of mouth-coating, yet fine Sangiovese tannin.

Metala White Label Shiraz / Cabernet 2006
Langhorne Creek
Australia

get it for...

$$$ ($21–30)

Nigel Dolan (1993 Jimmy Watson winner) is the man currently responsible for assembling Metala – one of Australia's favourite reds. Ironically, his late father, Bryan, won the inaugural Jimmy Watson in 1962 with the very same wine. Hailing from South Australia's Langhorne Creek, and with fruit still sourced from the original vineyard planted in 1891, Metala unleashes wave after wave of sweet plum and blackcurrant fruit together with aromas of mocha, bitter chocolate, and spice. In the mouth it's inky and rich with soft acidity and dry grippy tannins. It remains one of the planet's best buys.

Up and away (Part II)

I know it's not PC to admit so, but I love flying. Yes, I'm acutely aware of my responsibilities and as a result ride my bike whenever possible, catch the train when it's not, drive if I have to, and fly only when it's absolutely necessary. But it's not always that simple, and working for an organisation with venues either side of the equator, flying has become an integral part of my job. Call me strange, but the idea of sailing backward and forward from the UK to Australia three times a year doesn't exactly fill me with enthusiasm.

But, much as I enjoy climbing aboard a Jumbo, the effect of altitude on our senses is dramatic. Two things cause this. The first is the relatively low humidity of the cabin, that in turn affects our ability to smell, while low cabin pressure acts like anaesthetic on our taste-buds. As a result many wines will seem less fruity, more acidic, and higher in tannin than they appear on the ground. With this in mind, most airlines employ a crack team of experts who regularly sniff, swirl, and slurp their way through hundreds of wines in order to dig out the wines that perform best in the air.

Cooking is a brilliant way to learn more about wine. Getting your head around different smells, flavours, and textures in food will undoubtedly help you better understand what's going on in a glass of wine – not to mention giving you a major head start when it comes to pairing wine and food.

Get busy in the kitchen

Rymill Cabernet Sauvignon 2005
Coonawarra
Australia

John Innes has been the man behind the controls at Rymill since 1989, during which time he has turned out some stunning wines. From the near-perfect 2005 vintage, this is textbook Cabernet that definitely falls into the stunning camp. Concentrated, inky, and dense, the nose is loaded with aromas of cassis, leather, bitter chocolate, sweet spice, and mint. The palate is weighty and full, with loads of fruit and a brilliant structure. Best of all, the oak has been dealt out sparingly – and while the wine offers terrific drinking now, you could happily stash it under the bed for the better part of the next decade.

Peter Lehmann Margaret Barossa Semillon 2002

Barossa Valley
Australia

Named after the great Margaret Lehmann – wife of Peter, the champion of Barossa Semillon – "Margaret" has already gathered quite a collection of accolades in its debut year, including "Wine of the Competition" at the prestigious Sydney International Wine Competition 2008. Released with five years' age, this opens with a classic Semillon nose of ripe citrus fruit, honey, and spice. And expect to find a tight and firmly structured mouthful of wine that has real intensity of flavour, thanks to top shelf, old-vine Barossa fruit, alongside hints of smoke and spice. This is beautifully structured wine that, given the right conditions, will happily live on for the next decade and possibly beyond.

Australian stockists

Abbey Cellars
03 9690 5439

Amatos Liquor Mart
www.amatos.com.au

Armadale Cellars Fine Wines
www.armadalecellars.com.au

Arquilla Pty Ltd
www.arquilla.com

Auscellardoor
www.auscellardoor.com.au

Australian Wine Centre
www.auswine.com.au

Aussie Wines
www.aussiewines.com.au

Best Cellars
www.bestcellars.com.au

Bibendum (Australia)
www.bibendum.com.au (wholesale) /
www.ifw.com.au (retail)

Blackhearts & Sparrows
www.blackheartsandsparrows.com.au

Boccaccio Cellars
www.boccaccio.com.au

The Botanical Wine Store
www.winestore.net.au

Bottega Rotolo
www.bottegarotolo.com.au

Bottlemart
www.bottlemart.com.au

Brookvale Cellars
www.brookvalecellars.com.au

BWS (Beer, Wines, Spirits)
www.beerwinespirits

Cammeray Cellars
02 9955 2905

Canterbury Wines
www.canterburywines.net

Carlton Cellars
03 9380 1021

CBD Cellars
www.cbdcellars.com.au

Cellarbrations
www.cellarbrations.com.au

CellarHand
www.cellarhand.com.au

Chambers Cellars
www.chamberscellars.com.au

City Wine Shop
www.citywineshop.net.au

Coles
www.coles.com.au

Corporate Cellars
www.corporatecellars.net

Cru Bar + Cellar
www.crubar.com

Dan Murphy's
www.danmurphys.com.au

David Jones
www.davidjones-wineclub.com.au

David Matters Best Cellars Pty Ltd
02 9361 5454

Divino Cellars
03 9889 6988

D'Or to Door Wines Direct
www.dortodoor.com

Domaine Wine Shippers
www.dwssa.com.au

Drinx
07 3235 1887

East End Cellars
www.eastendcellars.com.au

Edinburgh Cellars
www.edinburgh.com.au

Euan McKay
www.euanmckay.com.au

Europa Cellars
www.europacellars.com.au

Fine Wine Partners
www.finewinepartners.com.au

First Choice
www.1stchoice.com.au

Five Ways Cellars
02 9360 4242

Fosters Group
www.fosters.com.au

Gertrude Street Enoteca
www.gertrudestreetenoteca.com

Hotel Cremorne Cellars
02 9909 8888

International Fine Wines
www.ifw.com.au

JHL Wine Co Pty Ltd
www.jhlwine.com

Jim's Cellars Waitara
www.jimscellars.com

Jim Murphy's Market Cellar
02 6295 0060

Kemenys
www.kemenys.com.au

King & Godfree
www.kingandgodfree.com.au

La Bergerie
03 9830 7915

La Vigna
www.lavigna.com.au

Lamb Wines
www.douglaslambwines.com.au

Leo's Fine Food & Wine
www.leos.com.au

Liquorland
www.liquorland.com.au

Lisa's Wine Vault
www.healthyUonline.com.au

Mosman Cellars
www.mosmancellars.com.au

Negociants
www.negociantsaustralia.com

Nicks Wine Merchants
www.nicks.com.au

Nillumbik Cellars
www.nillumbikcellars.com.au

North Sydney Cellars
www.northsydneycellars.com

Porter's Liquor
www.portersliquor.com.au

Prince Wine Store
www.princewinestore.com.au

Randall's
www.randalls.net.au

Rathdowne Cellars
www.rathdownecellars.com.au

Red + White
www.redandwhite.com.au

Re Store
08 9444 9644

Samuel Smith & Son
www.samsmith.com

Sixty Darling Street
02 9818 3077

The Spanish Acquisition
www.thespanishacquisition.com

Stephen McHenry Wine Merchants
www.stephenmchenrywinemerchant.
com.au

Stewarts Wine Co
www.stewartswineco.com.au

Strathmore Cellars
www.strath.com.au

Summer Hill Wine Shop
02 9798 7282

Tanunda Cellars
www.tanundacellars.com.au

Templestowe Cellars
www.templestowecellars.com.au

Trembath & Taylor
www.trembathandtaylor.com.au

Ultimo Wine Cellars
www.ultimowinecentre.com.au

Vaucluse Cellars
www.vauclusecellars.com.au

Vintage Blue
www.vintageblue.com.au

Vintage Cellars
www.vintagecellars.com.au

Wardens Food & Wine
www.wardens.com.au

Wine Bank on View
www.winebankonview.com

The Wine Emporium
www.australianwineemporium.com

Winelistaustralia
www.winelistaustralia.com

Woolworths
www.woolworths.com.au

New Zealand stockists

Note: Not all of the 100 recommended wines may be available through the retailers listed for New Zealand.

Accent on Wine (Auckland)
www.accentonwine.co.nz

Advintage (Hawkes Bay)
www.advintage.co.nz

Alberton Fine Foods (Auckland)
www.albertonwines.co.nz

Bacchus Cellars (Auckland)
www.bacchuscellars.co.nz

The Big Picture (Cromwell)
www.bigpicturewines.com

Blackmarket.co.nz (Auckland)
www.blackmarket.co.nz

The Cambridge Wine Company
(Cambridge)
www.cambridgewine.co.nz

Caros Wine Merchant (Auckland)
www.caros.co.nz

Central Otago Wine Cellars (Cromwell)
www.otagowine.com

Centre City Wine and Spirits (Wellington)
www.centrecity.co.nz

Don Johnsons (Auckland)
www.donjohnsons.co.nz

The Fine Wine Delivery Company
(Auckland)
www.finewinedelivery.co.nz

Finer Wines (Bay of Plenty)
+64 7 549 3463

First Glass (Auckland)
www.first-glass.co.nz

Glengarry (Auckland)
www.glengarry.co.nz

Hemingway Fine Wine
(Christchurch)
www.hemingwayfinewines.co.nz

Liquor King (Auckland)
www.liquorking.co.nz

Liquorland Fine Wines
(Auckland)
www.liquorlandfinewines.co.nz

Lovrich (Auckland)
www.lovrichwines.co.nz

Martinborough Wine Centre
(Martinborough)
www.martinboroughwinecentre.
co.nz

Meenan Wines & Spirits
(Dunedin)
www.meenans.co.nz

NZ Wine Specialist (Dunedin)
www.nzwinespecialist.co.nz

Regional Wines and Spirits
(Wellington)
www.regionalwines.co.nz

Scenic Cellars (Taupo)
www.sceniccellars.co.nz

St Heliers Bay Wines (Auckland)
www.stheliersbaywines.com

Vino Fino (Christchurch)
www.vinofino.co.nz

Wine Direct Imports (Auckland)
www.winedirect.co.nz

Wine Online (Auckland)
www.wineonline.co.nz

The Wine Vault (Auckland)
www.thewinevault.co.nz

Producer websites

Drink

A Mano
www.trembathandtaylor.com.au

Yalumba
www.yalumba.com

Coriole
www.coriole.com

Chapoutier
www.mchapoutieraustralia.com

Georges Duboeuf
www.duboeuf.com

Vinos de Telmo Rodríguez
www.thespanishacquisition.
com

Paxton
www.paxtonvineyards.com

De Bortoli
www.debortoli.com.au

Hewitson
www.hewitson.com.au

Plantagenet
www.plantagenetwines.com

Hugel
www.hugel.com

Water Wheel
www.waterwheelwine.com

Torres
www.torres.es

Primo Estate
www.primoestate.com.au

Dr Loosen
www.drloosen.com

Peter Lehmann
www.peterlehmannwines.
com.au

Two of a Kind
www.thomaswines.com.au

Jim Barry
www.jimbarry.com

Giesen
www.giesen.co.nz

T'Gallant
www.tgallant.com.au

Give

Coldstream Hills
www.coldstreamhills.com.au

Yarra Burn
www.yarraburn.com.au

Alkoomi
www.alkoomiwines.com.au

Brokenwood
www.brokenwood.com.au

Innocent Bystander
www.innocentbystander.com.au

Celler Capçanes
www.cellercapcanes.com

McHenry Hohnen
www.mchv.com.au

Penley Estate
www.penley.com.au

De Bortoli
www.debortoli.com.au

Bell Hill
www.bellhill.co.nz

Cullen
www.cullenwines.com.au

Ata Rangi
www.atarangi.co.nz

Archer
www.jhlwine.com

Henschke
www.henschke.com.au

Stella Bella
www.stellabella.com.au

d'Arenberg
www.darenberg.com.au

Kumeu River
www.kumeuriver.co.nz

Lillydale Estate
www.lillydaleestate.com.au

Wirra Wirra
www.wirra.com.au

Sutton Grange
www.suttongrangewines.com

Dine

Jansz
www.jansztas.com

Seppelt
www.seppelt.com.au

La Gitana
www.emiliohidalgo.es

Bress
www.bress.com.au

S C Pannell
www.scpannell.com.au

Donnafugata
www.donnafugata.it

Poggiotondo
www.poggiotondowines.com

Wild Rock
www.wildrockwine.co.nz

Garagiste
www.allies.com.au

Pondalowie Vineyards
www.pondalowie.com.au

Two Hands
www.twohandswines.com

Domaine de Durban
www.domainedurban.com

Lustau
www.emilio-lustau.com

Giant Steps
www.giant-steps.com.au

Stoneleigh
www.stoneleigh.co.nz

Muller-Catoir
www.mueller-catoir.de

Evans & Tate
www.evansandtate.com.au

Chalmers
www.chalmerswine.com.au

Primo Estate
www.primoestate.com.au

Escarpment
www.escarpment.co.nz

Splurge

Billecart-Salmon
www.champagne-billecart.fr

Egly-Ouriet
www.ifw.com.au

Mt Difficulty
www.mtdifficulty.co.nz

Roger Sabon
www.euanmckay.com.au

Vinedos Organicos Emiliana
www.emiliana.cl

Escarpment
www.escarpment.co.nz

Craiglee
www.craiglee.com.au

Bouchard Père et Fils
www.bouchard-pereetfils.com

Kooyong
www.kooyong.com

Paul Jaboulet Ainé
www.jaboulet.com

Domaine Leflaive
www.leflaive.fr

Arrivo
08 8370 8072

Grattamacco
www.trembathandtaylor.com.au

Henriques & Henriques
www.henriquesehenriques.pt

Giaconda
www.giaconda.com.au

Pierre Morey
morey-blanc@wanadoo.fr

Highbank
www.highbank.com.au

Planeta
www.planeta.it

Tscharke
www.redandwhite.com.au

Clonakilla
www.clonakilla.com.au

Stash

Delamotte
www.jhlwine.com

Fonseca
www.fonsecaport.com

Taylors
www.taylorswines.com.au

Tyrrell's
www.tyrrells.com.au

McWilliams
www.mcwilliams.com.au

Pizzini
www.pizzini.com.au

Robinvale
www.organicwines.com.au

Quartz Reef
www.quartzreef.co.nz

De Bortoli
www.debortoli.com.au

William Fevre
www.williamfevre.fr

Sorrenberg
www.sorrenberg.com

Shadowfax
www.shadowfax.com.au

Cape Mentelle
www.capementelle.com.au

Dry River
www.dryriver.co.nz

Tahbilk
www.tahbilk.com.au

Pyramid Valley
www.pyramidvalley.com

Isole e Olena
www.negociantsaustralia.com

Metala
www.fosters.com.au

Rymill
www.rymill.com.au

Peter Lehmann
www.peterlehmannwines.
  com.au

Cheers

For Carls & Indi xx

Another year and another raft of people to thank for helping bring this edition of *The Juice* to life – here goes…

First up to Chris Terry, Matt Utber, and their respective teams: Jade, Lisa, and all the crew at The Plant, and Danny Tracy at Chris Terry Photography – massive thanks and respect for tireless efforts, good ideas and help, but mostly just for putting up with Chris. To my team: Debbie Catchpole and Verity O'Brien at Fresh Partners and Lisa Sullivan at One Management. To all the gang at Mitchell Beazley: Alison Goff, David Lamb, Hilary Lumsden, Becca Spry, Leanne Bryan, Fiona Smith, Tim Foster, Yasia Williams-Leedham and, in the same breath, Louise Sherwin-Stark and Kate Taperell at Hachette Australia. Huge love and thanks to you all. To my extended family: Fifteen Group (London, Cornwall, Amsterdam, and Melbourne), Jonathan Downey and Match Group (London, Ibiza, New York, Charmonix, and Melbourne), Frank van Haandel and Roger Fowler, Trevor Eastment at XYZ Networks, William Sitwell at *Waitrose Food Illustrated*, and Nick Scott at *GQ Australia*. And last but not least, to those behind the scenes including my amazing Mum (x), my brother Drew, Caroline, Jessie, Eve, Anne, Thommo, Gin, Camilla and Felix, Tobe, George, Randy, Pip, Gyros, BP, CC, and GG, Jamie and Jools, Danny McCubbin, David Gleave, Philip Rich, Stuart Gregor, Cam Mackenzie, Andy Frost, The Jones, Cooper-Terry, and Utber clans, Scania at Howies, Kate at Adidas Originals, Lucas and Indigo at Odo for keeping me awake with some of the best coffee south of the river, Dan Holland at Victoria Bitter, The Mighty Hawks, and beautiful Melbourne town.

M x